BREAKING PROTOCOL

BREAKING PROTOCOL

MARIA HUPFIELD

INVENTORY PRESS

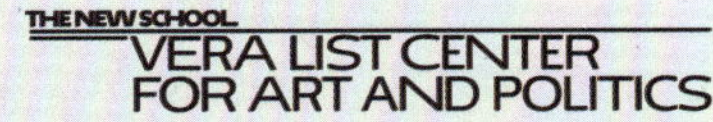

MARIA HUPFIELD

INTRODUCTION

In 2020 at the height of the COVID-19 pandemic, I began to host Coffee Break, an extended series of private Zoom conversations that brought together a selection of performance artists from diverse Indigenous Nations comprised of Native Americans (United States), First Nations, Metis, Inuit (Canada), and Native Pacific Islanders. I hosted these conversations from my home studio in Toronto, Ontario, setting in motion a dramatic shift in the focus of my inaugural Borderlands Fellowship (2020–2022) with the Vera List Center for Art and Politics at The New School (New York) and the Center for Imagination in the Borderlands at Arizona State University (Tempe, Arizona).

The Coffee Break sessions coincided with a moment during the pandemic when public presentations moved out of institutions and into domestic and studio spaces. It represented a new reality in which conversations—and performances—in front of live public audiences were not possible. Reflecting on this moment, we recognized the necessity of providing ourselves space to speak about our work, in private conversations, on our own terms, and as artists dedicated to the performance form from vastly different Nations, we needed to connect, across borders and continents.

Applying a standard of ethical collaborative processes adapted from my own performance practice and artistic protocols, I invited each artist to offer a series of private, group-led, one-hour conversations with four to six artists. A total of thirty-five people participated. These sessions were not exhaustive, but captured a cross section of the rich diversity, range, and scope of Indigenous artists and thinkers based on a network of personal connections from a moment in time. This process is one that is reflective of my personal arts practice, which focuses on strength in diversity in an effort to move away from scarcity models in the visual arts.

This book is a response to the feeling of alienation that united many of us during the pandemic and the ongoing lack of resources afforded to Indigenous performance artists. That said, this work was made possible through the generous support of the Borderlands Fellowship. My goal was to center relation building, to serve as a sort of mental health or well-being check in, and to sit in community during a period of time when in-person performances came to a full stop. Gratitude to the artists in this publication for their work and trust, Yuki Kihara for being a bridge and connector, Natalie Diaz for her intellectual rigor and fire, Dr. Jennifer Wemegwans, Jason Lujan, my research assistant Amanda Berardi, and Re’al Christian, Assistant Director of Editorial Initiatives at the Vera List Center, as well as the entire VLC team.

Building on the Coffee Break sessions, *Breaking Protocol* is my gift to honor the strength and beauty of so many artists who fuel and feed my practice; it comes from the desire to hold space together, connect, continue, resist, feed the spirit, and thrive! Throughout these exchanges, the artists demonstrate their diversity of practices, their grounding in Indigenous knowledge, and their collective approaches to demanding sovereignty and critical accountability. Conversations on themes of language, artistic process, sexuality, loss, and joy proliferate, as participants discuss performance—or the performative—as both theory and practice.

Bridging the gap between the personal and the political, the individual and the institutional, this publication asks: How do we translate performance as a living art form to book form while avoiding the pitfalls of the archive as a static object? What stories become political agents in the liberation of the archive from its colonial underpinnings and structure? What can we learn from Indigenous artistic protocols of making and practice that open spaces for reciprocity and multiplicity?

I invite you to keep this book on your coffee table to savor. I promise it will be good until the last drop.

TANYA LUKIN LINKLATER

SENSATION

Sensation is a circuit of experience, a circuit of the felt traveling in and adjacent to the body.

The sensation. Of edges of density—to recall.
Of edges of dissipation—to breathe. Edges.
This is where Sugpiaq come into being. At the
edges of imaq, nuna, lla, these spaces between.

The edges of history. The edges of surrender. The edges of violence. The edge.

What happens when we recall (harden)?
What happens when we surrender to dissipation,
breath (being)?
Is restoration a transformation of that which
can harden us, into breath?
Restoration of our being, a surrender to
dissipation.

*   *   *   *   *

Colonialisms are continuous actions; they are daily. They refuse Indigenous sovereignty. They seek to remove us from our lands, to dispossess us. They seek land and resources; their mode is extractive. They extract children from our families; they extract our ancestral and cultural belongings and ancestors' remains from our homelands and peoples. Ongoing colonialisms, settler and otherwise, dehumanize. They are multiple. They attempt to disappear us. They extract, remove, contain, and suspend our ideas. Colonialisms are systemic—a series of ideas that come to be embodied in everyday actions, in interactions, in relations, in institutions. They are felt.

*   *   *   *   *

When Inupiaq, Yup'ik, or Sugpiaq singers stretch hide on drums, it moves. It is moved. Misted water droplets are rubbed into it with circular motions. Hands pull it tighter around a wooden edge. We strike this edge gently with sticks made for sound. As a material it expands, entering space as vibration. It responds to what it is being asked to do. Its form and materiality shift. We call it and, in its response, hide (the skin of a sea or land mammal) is transformative. Hide is an edge.

* * * * *

Like hide, gut has many lives. Gut was once in the belly of an animal. Worked by the hands of women, a preparation for its subsequent life. Like hide, it is cleaned, scraped, wrung, dried, tanned. Gut is a geometry of many strips sewn together watertight to clothe and shelter us. Gut breathes. Gut is stitched, plumed, painted, marked. Gut is adorned. Gut moves with us, protects us from sea salt spray and wind on ocean current. Gut expands and contracts with the weather. It expands with warm touch. Gut is worn by hunters, medicine people, and women dancing nude underneath. Gut is transparent. Gut reflects then fills with light shimmering. When we place gut in museums without sea-salt air, it hardens, brittles. Its ossification withers seams. Immobile and stacked in dark stale cupboards, it is rarely held or sounded. It tears over time. The forms of ancestral and cultural belongings change with the weather.

Twentieth-century Yankton Dakota writer and activist Zitkála-Šá describes shorn telegraph poles, still. No longer breathing or moved by wind. Electrical impulses pumped through their bodies. In her writings, she wonders about the life of these trees before they became a tool of white settler expansion. An ever-growing coded communication across her homelands, the prairies. She imagines many Indigenous children as forests that become shorn, milled into timber in service of white systems. She is implicated in these systems as a former student and teacher in Indian boarding schools. Yet she imagines and remembers the life of trees before they ever became telegraph poles. And she senses within the poles an older life force.

PETER MORIN

TAHLTAN KNOWLEDGE AS A FORM OF LANGUAGE PERFORMANCE: REFLECTIONS ON MY BEGINNINGS WITH INDIGENOUS PERFORMANCE ART

p. 19
Peter Morin, *Circle*, 2010. Presented at the University of British Columbia. Photos by Stephen Foster, courtesy of the artist.

Performance art called to me when I was a recent art school graduate. I was broke. I couldn't afford the fees for a printmaking studio. I needed something that could fit in my pocket and could travel with me, if/when I got some sort of art-related job. This wasn't, and would never be, the marble lithography stones I trained to make artwork with at art school.

My first performance happened in 2005 at the New Forms Festival. This opportunity began as a challenge from curator Karen Benbassat Ali. She approached me on the street and said, "I want to see what you can do to challenge museum polemics." My second performance happened in 2007 at the Royal Ontario Museum, and it only happened because the curators, Candice Hopkins and Kerry Swanson, had heard about the earlier performance at New Forms. I deepened my performance practice in 2009 with *12 Making Objects: 12 Indigenous Interventions AKA First Nations DADA* at Open Space, and again in 2011 with *Peter Morin's Museum*, a series of performances and evolving installations. This practice developed further when I started a collaborative performance with my best friend Ayumi Goto in 2013. Sometimes, I think I became a real "performance artist" in 2009, but then I remember a quiet performance that happened in my art school days in the late nineties. I asked Daina Warren to help me. I wanted to project slides of Tahltan history onto our Indigenous bodies. Tahltan people have territory found/located in northern British Columbia (BC). We are Dene.

I completed my master's degree in 2010 with an exhibition entitled *Circle*. My research reflected an increasing awareness of the very real body sensation I was feeling when trying to speak the limited Tahltan words I knew in the environments I was living in. In my thesis document, I used the phrase "psychological blockage," but in reality it felt like a physical wall, one that stopped the didenek'eh from leaving my mouth. My two and a half years of research led to a series of interconnected performances that took place over ten days at the FINA gallery, at the University of British Columbia Okanagan Art Gallery in Kelowna. These seven interlocking performances were called: *Letters to my Grandmother*; *Billy Jack goes to Washington*; *A Hunting Party*; *3 forms of Tahltan knowledge AKA a Tahltan genealogy of knowledge or what I am doing here*; *A Sweatlodge at the Bottom of the Stikine River*; *Reading the old testament translated into Gwitch'in to River Stones*; and finally *A Circle for my Thesis Defence*. The performances were designed to mirror Tahltan knowledge(s) in practice and to build an experience for Tahltan knowing. I did stray far from my research intentions to understand what factors, in the urban environments that I was existing in, were informing/shaping that "psychological blockage" that was keeping me from Tahltan language speaking/practice.

My parents play a role in this work as well. My mom, Janell, is Tahltan. My dad, Pierre, is French Canadian. We grew up in northern BC, close to our reserve. While growing up, our mom made sure that we were very connected to old school Tahltan elders. This meant that I was often inside of Tahltan language fluent environments. This doesn't mean that these elders were speaking with me, it means I was there in the room. I could see how my grandmothers were talking Tahltan and moving their bodies while talking/listening to the spoken and performed Tahltan meaning. Like so many of our community members, we also grew up with the heavy spectre of the Indian residential schools in these rooms.

In my research, in looking for guidance from fluent language speakers, linguistics, Tahltan elders, elders, artists, global artists, I realized that Indigenous language speaking lives and emerges from multiple sites of knowing/practice and doesn't rest solely within a spoken voice. One of the main sites of the practice of speaking is the body. Another site for speaking language is the artwork created by Indigenous artists. Performance art became a means for me to practice Tahltan Nation knowledge(s) in environments that weren't necessarily tied to the territory. Positioning performance in this way allowed me to practice Tahltan knowledge in ways that spoke to my world with no limitations or forced silences.

The following visual and written offerings include elements of my thesis research and exhibition completed in 2010. My performance(s), and performance planning, are still deeply invested in what I learned from this research. This performative reading starts with my language acknowledgment: "Hello. My name is Ezek-Tah. My Tahltan family is from Telegraph Creek, Dease Lake, and Iskut. My Tahltan family was born in Telegraph Creek, Dease Lake, and Iskut. Good Day. I'm going to tell you a story. My name is Ezek-Tah. I am a young language speaker and I don't speak Tahltan very well."

Duda-antini
Ezeck-tah Onye
Es Didene T'sini Tlegohin, Tat-lah, Kluwecheon nande
Es Didene Dendatah Tle gohin, Tat-lah, Kluwecheon nande
Dzene s hoti'e
Tsedze susahts'a n
EzekTah ushye
E, diden tsedle usehs'an
Edu didene K'eh soga hodese
—Peter Morin, excerpt from artist statement, "An unofficial history of Tahltan epistemology 2010."

I've spent time in performance putting my own brown body in the center of the space. I've investigated, mapped out, and dismantled what I was calling the impact zone that happens when Western settler colonialism and Indigenous knowledge(s) collide on the land. I've thought/practiced/taught about decolonizing gestures and the radical opening of unimagined space/possibilities that occurs when these gestures are performed in sequence and with intention. I've investigated the power of risk through performance. I've also learned about the power/agency of the brown body to open space for Ancestors through performance art. In my collaborative work with Ayumi Goto over the past eight years, we have made agreements to honor each other's Ancestors and Mothers first. We have also turned increasingly towards joy as a creative material that is more powerful than colonization. I have turned decolonizing methodologies inward through performance to decolonizing my heart, liver, lungs, stomach. I've also become more interested in, and am prioritizing, Indigenous power. I've had the privilege of being trained by James Luna, Adrian Stimpson, Cheryl L'Hirondelle, Guillermo Gómez-Peña, VestAndPage, and Rebecca Belmore. I come to this work because of the incredible offerings/trail breaking of Rebecca Belmore. Her work, her efforts, her strength teach us that we may not have access to all the spoken language of our Ancestors, but we always have our bodies and our body's ability to move with strength.

Performance art as a research methodology happened because I wanted to be closer into Tahltan Nation Language speaking/knowledge/practice. I wanted to understand Tahltan ideas and their relationship to Tahltan epistemology. In 2007, I had moved from a very northern Indigenous location to a place where there were no other Tahltan people around to speak with. Watson Lake, Yukon to Victoria, British Columbia. I decided that something was keeping me from practicing spoken Tahltan in the city. I found that I was even scared to speak the words, and I wanted to know why. I also found that I started to lose the words I had fought so hard to gain. In support of finding the answer, I applied for a master's program and focused my research towards investigating that wall/blockage—that energy that was keeping me from speaking/sharing our Tahltan language. This essay is filled with excerpts from my thesis, *Circle* (2010). In this text, I have written down—attempted to articulate—my dreamings about language, language speaking, and its connection to performance. In my MFA research, and the accompanying exhibition, I performed six times over a ten-day period, and each performance transitioned the experience of knowing/practicing Tahltan knowledge(s) as well as the installation. These performances were designed around Tahltan knowledge as a form of language speaking. These days I'm still thinking about, and reflecting on how formational this work was and continues to be as I continue my work as a Tahltan Nation performance artist. I think it's important to include these ideas here as offerings; they are still informing and influencing my thinking, as well as my body movements in performance. *Please note that the original thesis was written eleven years ago, and I have since decided to change all the lowercase spellings of "indigenous" to "Indigenous."

Excerpts from *Circle* concerning performance art and the embodiment of Tahltan meaning/language/ideas:

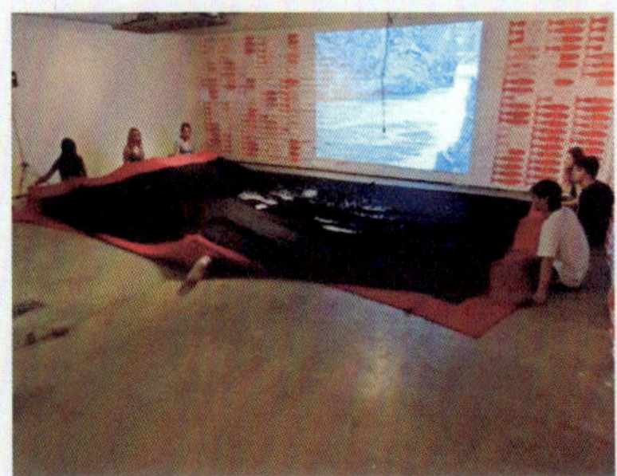

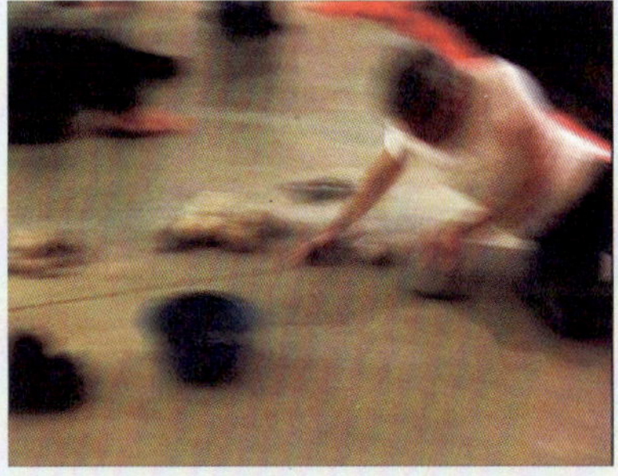

As a Tahltan Nation person I found that I was able to perform general Tahltan ways of knowing but unable to elevate this performance through spoken language. In Tahltan language speaking I was able to speak twenty words of spoken Tahltan; however, in my performance of Tahltan meaning, I was able to make button blankets, drums, and birch bark baskets, do bead work, organize a potlatch, and speak my family tree.

Language is a system of Indigenous meaning, and the performance of that meaning in community creates a legacy of relational knowing and new culture.

My grandmother, as a living and breathing member of the community, has a sense of language that speaks to a body of knowledge that lives in relation to the other physical Tahltan bodies who have an innate ability to perform Tahltan meaning. Our capacity to acknowledge the relational aspects connected to Indigenous ways of knowing is the key to development and performance of Tahltan meaning and survival.

Raven did not know how to cut up salmon. He defecated and asked his excrements for advice. As soon as they began to speak, he held up his hand and said, "Hush! I know." However, as soon as he began to cut the fish, he forgot what he had been told and asked again. This happened many times in succession.

Meaning (i.e., the provision of food for the community, the development of hunting knowledge within a family), defined by Indigenous ways of knowing (i.e., the places and ways we have always hunted), continues to exist after the performance (i.e., the telling of the story of the hunt), and reperformance (the retelling of the story of the hunt) of the event. This is an age-old process.

As an artist, a maker of objects, and a future fluent speaker of the Tahltan language, I choose to privilege the created object and subsequent performance of meaning connected to the making of that object as an example of spoken language.

To be successful at performing Tahltan meaning, we have to develop strategies which help us to articulate collectively responsive relationships to colonial systems of power. We continue to move on the land which remains a much older practice of knowledge making and production than the western practices.

An important performance in the Tahltan creation story is the act of giving the light. This significant gift and the act of giving so freely is another key demonstration of Tahltan ways of knowing.

I've re-edited the published version to reflect the performative nature of our spoken Tahltan language and our Grandma Eva's storytelling.

I have focused on these non-verbal creative practices as a way to recreate experiential knowledge connected to spoken language and performance of meaning.

There is also creating a strategy or a process for organizing the experiential learning that results from the making and completion of an object. Language speaking is a challenge. The communication of meaning, the cultural performance of meaning, and the speaking of language require practice, patience, and initiation into a culture of meaning making.

It always meant something to me, that first time I danced in our home community. Our cousin Johnny Frank was there. He was still alive. We were at the community school in Telegraph Creek. My grandmother was still alive. I can't remember what we were actually dancing for but I can remember the dancing.

And when he danced in, he made a shape with his hands like a bird. I remember him checking in with an Elder in the room to make sure that this hand position was correct. And for some reason I remember someone saying this hand shape was a chickadee.

My dancing was speaking to her. The dancing was saying something to our grandmother. I was speaking the language of Tahltan meaning through my movements. I was performing a cultural history which connected me to our community, to our family, to our nation, to the history of ideas, and to our grandmother. I felt good about the dancing. I wasn't shy. I wasn't worried about making mistakes.

A good basket collects food and our younger siblings can eat. A bad basket spills the food and our little sister goes hungry. A poorly made basket breaks and means no one gets to eat. We made baskets to hold our stories. These baskets carry these stories and help develop our ways of knowing.

When you are speaking your language you are making something. Your speaking becomes a small contribution to the survival of your community. And you are allowed to do this. You have to give yourself permission to speak and perform Indigenous meaning. Make no apologies.

Our bodies are creating and demonstrating new Indigenous meaning as defined by community-based art practices and values.

We love to dance to Tahltan country music. Our cousins are the best musicians in the world. They can sing the old country music, and the old gospel songs. When these songs are sung to a large gathered Tahltan audience in our community, angels come down to join us.

Our stories continually transformed and were consistently being redefined by our speaking with Indigenous meaning. The speaking of our language also allowed us to envision a space outside of this classroom, where we could bring this spoken language back to our homes, families, and elders.

I believe that spoken language is a created object. It has structure which implies physicality. This physicality is engaged through the body. Language is connected to the history of knowledge and ideas within its specific community of origin. The act of speaking my language is an act of performing meaning, history, and ideas. The act of speaking this history, organized as language, creates a connection for both the speaker and the listener to the history of knowledge and ideas within its specific community of origin.

Indigenous artists shape forms which support the practice of investigating knowledge defined by Indigenous ways of knowing and are able to transform space through the performance of that recovered, experienced, articulated Indigenous meaning.

The Tahltan meaning resulting from the performance of these Tahltan words also has a profound and transformational effect on the space. The performance of Tahltan meaning, as a Tahltan practice, rearranges space, time, and history within a gallery space that is dominated by Western perspectives. The meaning attached to the performance of these Tahltan words changes and deepens in relationship to a location transforming our relationship and understanding of the physical space.

Performance art and performance of Indigenous meaning should be read as two separate but connected entities. Both artists and speakers of language, as organizers of knowledge, have a responsibility to effectively represent their connection to epistemological truths and practice. We also continue to create meaning which contributes to the overall well-being of the epistemological body.

This piece is called *there is a circle at the bottom of the river/meaning happens at the bottom of the river/un-official history of epistemological practices of the Tahltan Nation*. These spoken words, and performance, will organize itself into the space. I will have prepared objects which will act as transmitters of energy connected to the Tahltan Indigenous meaning that I am representing. These objects will carry this Tahltan meaning throughout the space.

I blindfold myself and climb under the edge of the button blanket. This button blanket covers the entire floor of the gallery. It reaches from wall to wall. It is its own gallery representing Tahltan meaning. It is huge but still moves like a button blanket should move. A button blanket should flow like the river.

There are buttons on top of the blanket. They are not fixed to the blanket. Their movement makes a sound like the river.
—Peter Morin, excerpt from artist statement, "An unofficial history of Tahltan epistemology 2010."

The hunter tells the story of the hunt. The hunter tells the story so that we will listen. We sit together and talk about the hunter's experience. We sit together and talk about these new experiences. And we share the meat that was brought back.

We stopped reading the words, or reciting the words, and created the words in the classroom. At one point, we became black bears, grizzly bears, groundhogs, wolves, crows, rabbits, and a herd of caribou. We acknowledged our history and hunted for language that is for everyone.

The words can sound too big for your mouth. The meaning attached to the spoken word can fall out of your mouth and hit the ground hard. Be careful but don't be afraid of your language. Have some fun with speaking. Make jokes to hear elders laugh.

As an urban-based Tahltan person and language learner, if I couldn't find another Tahltan person to speak the language with, I could still speak the language of meaning through performance and performance exchange.

WORK CITED

Morin, Peter. *Circle*. University of British Columbia, MFA Thesis, 2010. https://go.exlibris.link/gpR1kJVB.

WANDA NANIBUSH

THE SOUND OF THE COLOUR FIELD: ON REBECCA BELMORE

pp. 30–33
Rebecca Belmore, *The Sound of the Colour Field*, 2022. Presented by aabaakwad 2022 at Ocean Space, Venice, Italy, April 23, 2022. Photos courtesy of the artist.

In April 2022, Rebecca Belmore and I traveled to Venice, Italy, to prepare for an original performance marking two occasions: aabaakwad 2022—an international gathering of Indigenous artists, curators, and writers I started in 2018—and Belmore's return to the Venice Biennale after representing Canada in 2005.

The site I had procured was a beautiful deconsecrated ninth-century church in Campo San Lorenzo that became a contemporary arts venue in 2019 called Ocean Space, one of aabaakwad's collaborators. Belmore had an inspired idea already brewing when we talked at her opening in New York at the Whitney Biennial a few days before. She wanted to use multiple colored fabrics to create an abstract image, a color field painting, like a painter would use oils. But one thing that can never be produced in a painting that can in a performance is sound. The main action of the work would be the ripping of one thousand yards of fabric—enough to "paint" the courtyard from the steps of the church to the water well in the center. The strips of material were laid out in color blocks—reds, oranges, blues, greens, and whites moving from blood to sunsets to skies, earth and water, gradually revealing a final abstract landscape. Sixteen artists in aabaakwad stood in the courtyard tearing the fabric for forty-five minutes, the noise inspiring the work's title, *The Sound of the Colour Field*.[1] I must digress at this point to discuss the space. Belmore is a master at drawing out deep meaning from the spaces her work occupies and engages.

The church of San Lorenzo is notable as the resting place of Venetian explorer Marco Polo. For centuries it has been admired as a picturesque site of worship for Roman Catholics, as well as a home for Benedictine monks. For many Indigenous people, the church signifies and memorializes the traumatic history of the violent Christianization of over one hundred fifty

1 Matti Aikio, Tony Albert, Mosab Alnomire, Paschal Berry, Daniel Browning, Dayna Danger, Jeremy Dutcher, Harald Gaski, Brett Graham, Gunvor Guttorm, Greg Hill, Ursula Johnson, Michelle LaVallee, Rod Nanibush, Sage Paul, Rachael Rekana, and aqui Thami.

years of ~~Indian~~[2] Residential schools (IRS).[3] A great global reckoning has begun where the crimes against our children over so many generations are finally being unearthed; the apologies keep coming, most recently from Pope Francis.[4] Sitting on the steps of Campo San Lorenzo, Belmore and I spoke about the recent actions to memorialize and mourn the Indigenous children who were being found in mass and unmarked graves on IRS grounds across Canada. We both thought of the women in our families, their strength and pain.

As we looked at the square, which is bordered by a canal, we also spoke about Belmore's 2005 work *Fountain*, a sixteen-foot wall of water onto which a video is projected. The video has water turn into blood and blood into water. *Fountain* was a prescient work that spoke to water as a source of a future war, but also as a site of responsibility and resistance. In the intervening years since she made that work, her vision has become clear; many activist movements such as Idle No More and Standing Rock, to name only two, have similarly made water protection central to their work.

The steps in front of the desacralized church became the starting point of her performance and color choices.

On April 23 at 7 pm, the sky opened up in a soft, cold rain, magically mirroring what I and maybe a hundred other Indigenous artists and three hundred guests at the Venice Biennale were feeling. I let tears slide down my cheeks because they were indistinguishable from the rain while holding/hugging two friends in comfort and warmth. The performance hit me hard right away (even though I knew what was coming). The sight of sixteen bodies ripping red

2 I strikethrough the word ~~Indian~~ because it is in the actual name for the schools but still a misnomer—the strikethrough marks the conundrum of history and language.

3 To learn more about IRS and the Truth and Reconciliation Commission, see: https://nctr.ca/about/history-of-the-trc/truth-and-reconciliation-commission-of-canada.

4 Read the Pope's full apology for the Catholic Church's role in IRS here: https://www.ctvnews.ca/canada/read-the-full-text-of-pope-francis-speech-and-apology-1.6001384.

fabric in front of the church made me think of the rivers of blood that have flowed from these places of worship and how they stole so many childhoods. I thought of my mother attending one of these prisons masquerading as Christian benevolence and improvement. It was the amplified sound of tearing nylon fabric that brought me simultaneously into a feeling of the power of creation alongside grief. Belmore chose to start the performance with red fabric to evoke blood, but also red power and sunsets as the progression of colors shifted into orange. Beauty with grief is Belmore's trademark. As her workers moved to new colors and onto the square each of them started to individualize their motions, and eventually they started working together. Each body became part of a choreography with Belmore as the master choreographer directing both their movements and the building of the image through color. In the final action they surrounded the well where Belmore joined them in what felt like a prayer to the water. The deep love we have for water and land has only ever been strengthened by the violence that has tried to rip it from us.

The Sound of the Colour Field in the year 2022 was a visualization of the turmoil, trauma, and daily work we are doing on behalf of our lost and murdered children and the first mother we must protect.

As the square emptied, I marveled at the beauty of the painting Belmore had produced from strips of nylon. In a space like the Venice Biennale, the critique was also clear—Belmore drew upon human fragility, vulnerability, and emotion to create her own color field, dismissing the modernist and ethnocentric art world on display at the biennale.

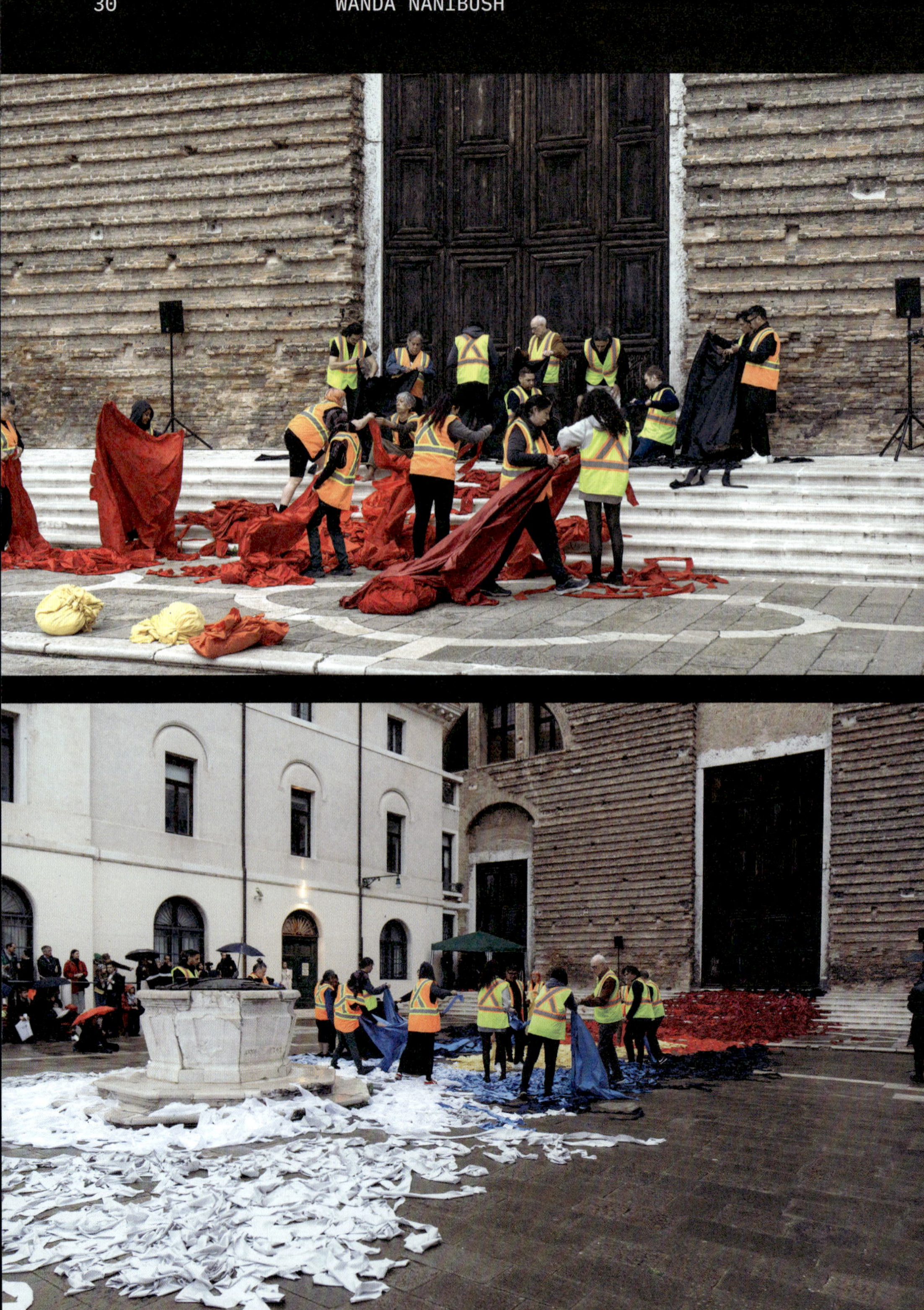

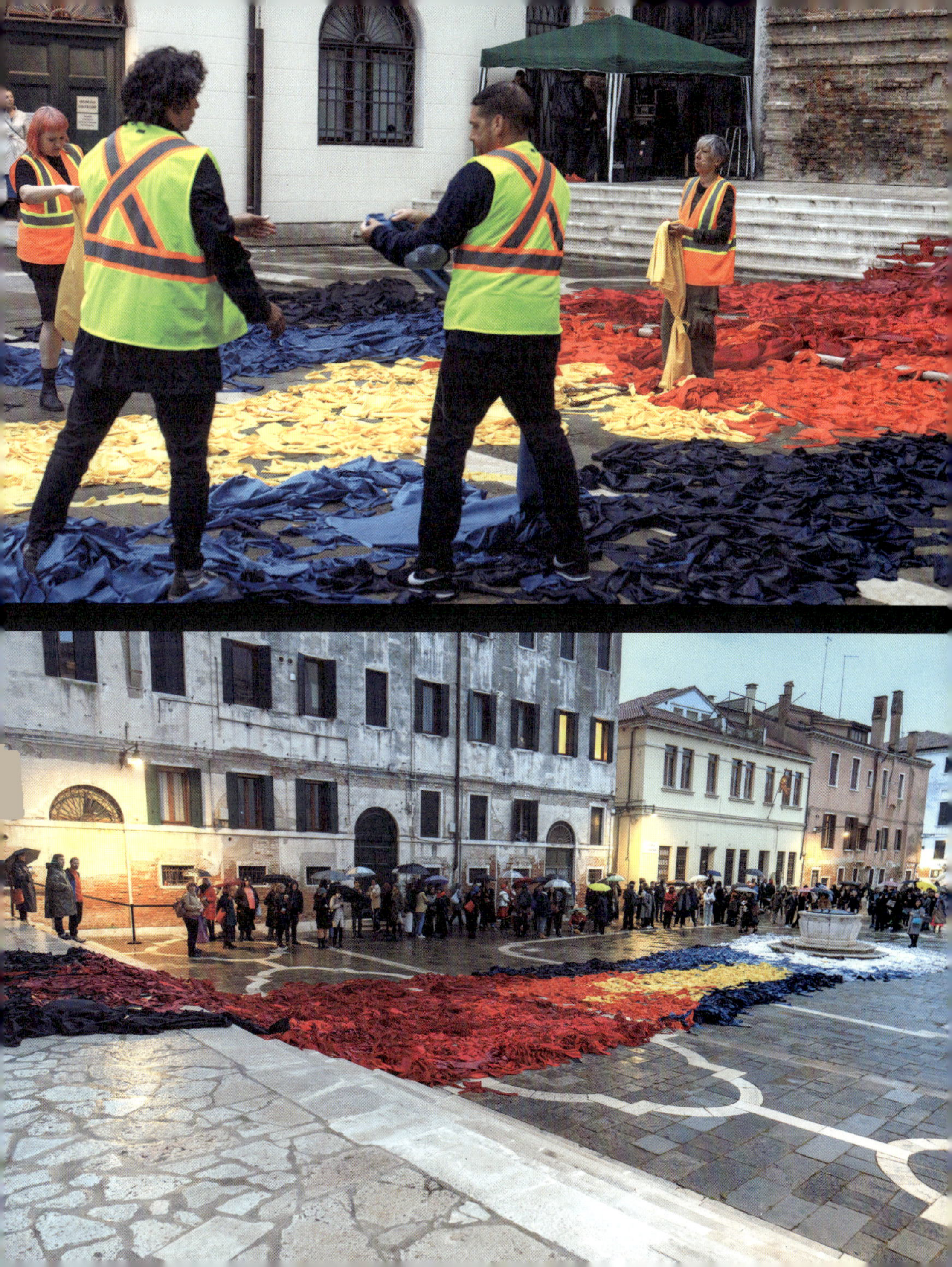

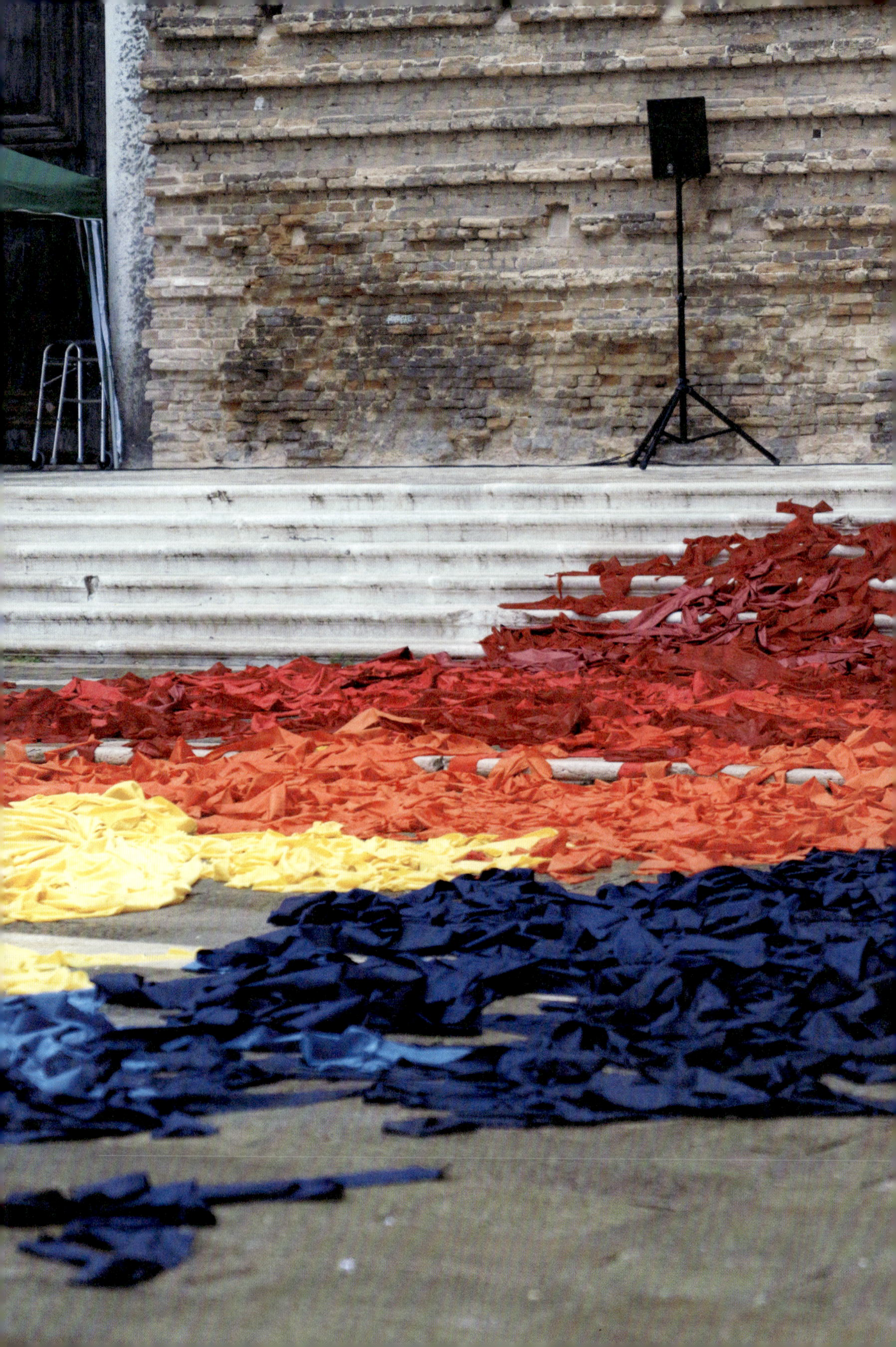

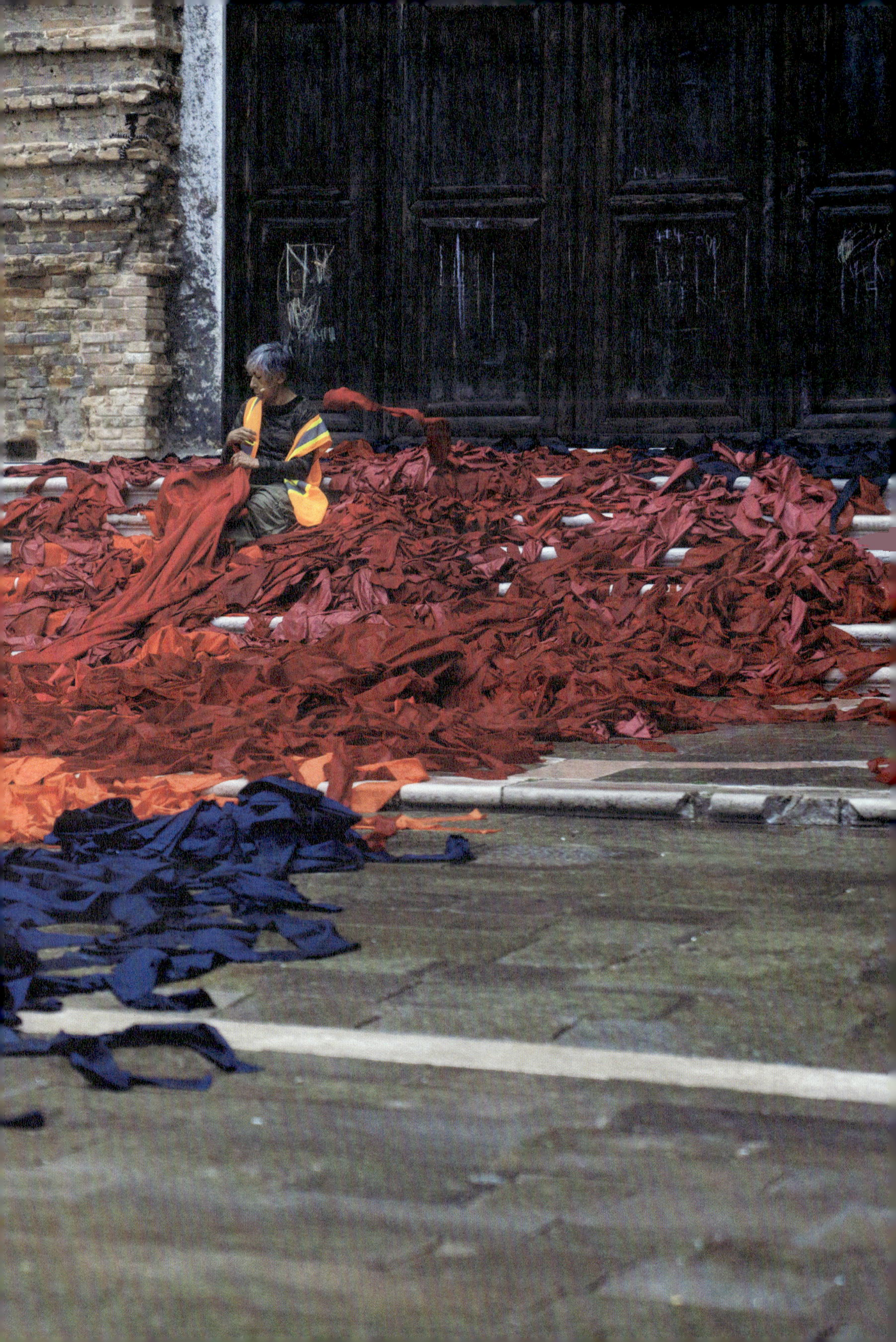

MEAGAN MUSSEAU

COUSINS

With an artistic practice that spans new media, land-based performances, installations, and video, Meagan Musseau's innovative coalescence of natural and commercially made materials pushes conversations about access to resources and land. Her performance *Cousins* features a material activation—a neon-hued pendant trudged through the snow calls our attention to the stark contrast of the synthetic and the organic, the material and the land, while highlighting the interrelatedness and kinship between all beings in the soft encounter between these seemingly disparate materials. With *Cousins*, Musseau uses fabricated material modifications as an act of survivance in which she perseveres in nurturing her culture by fostering a generative relationship between materials and the land.

pp. 35–37
Meagan Musseau, land-based activation of *Cousins*, with bear paw snowshoes and orange ribbon fringe walking through "crown land remote license lot 18" on unceded Ktaqmkuk territory for video, 2021. Photos courtesy of the artist.

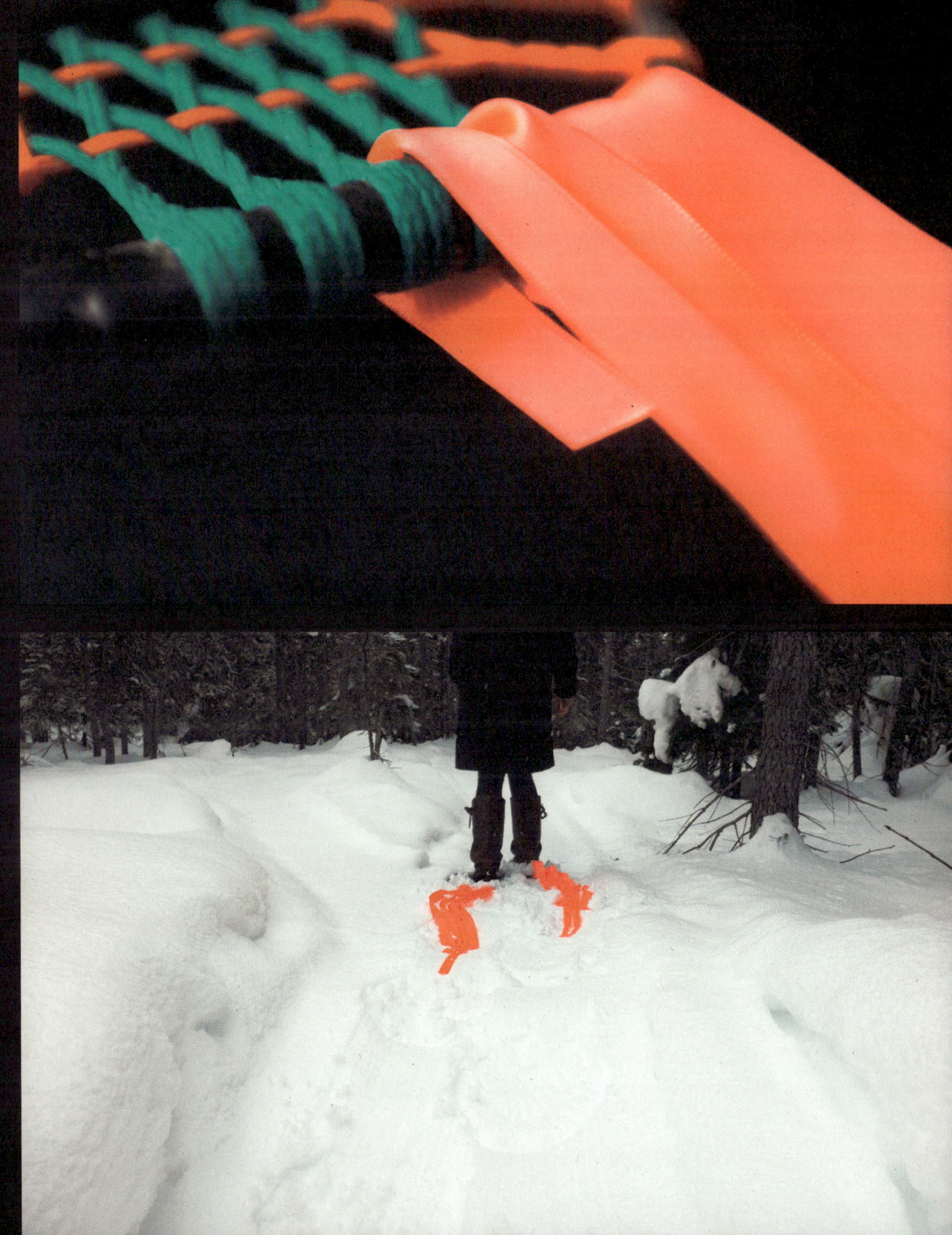

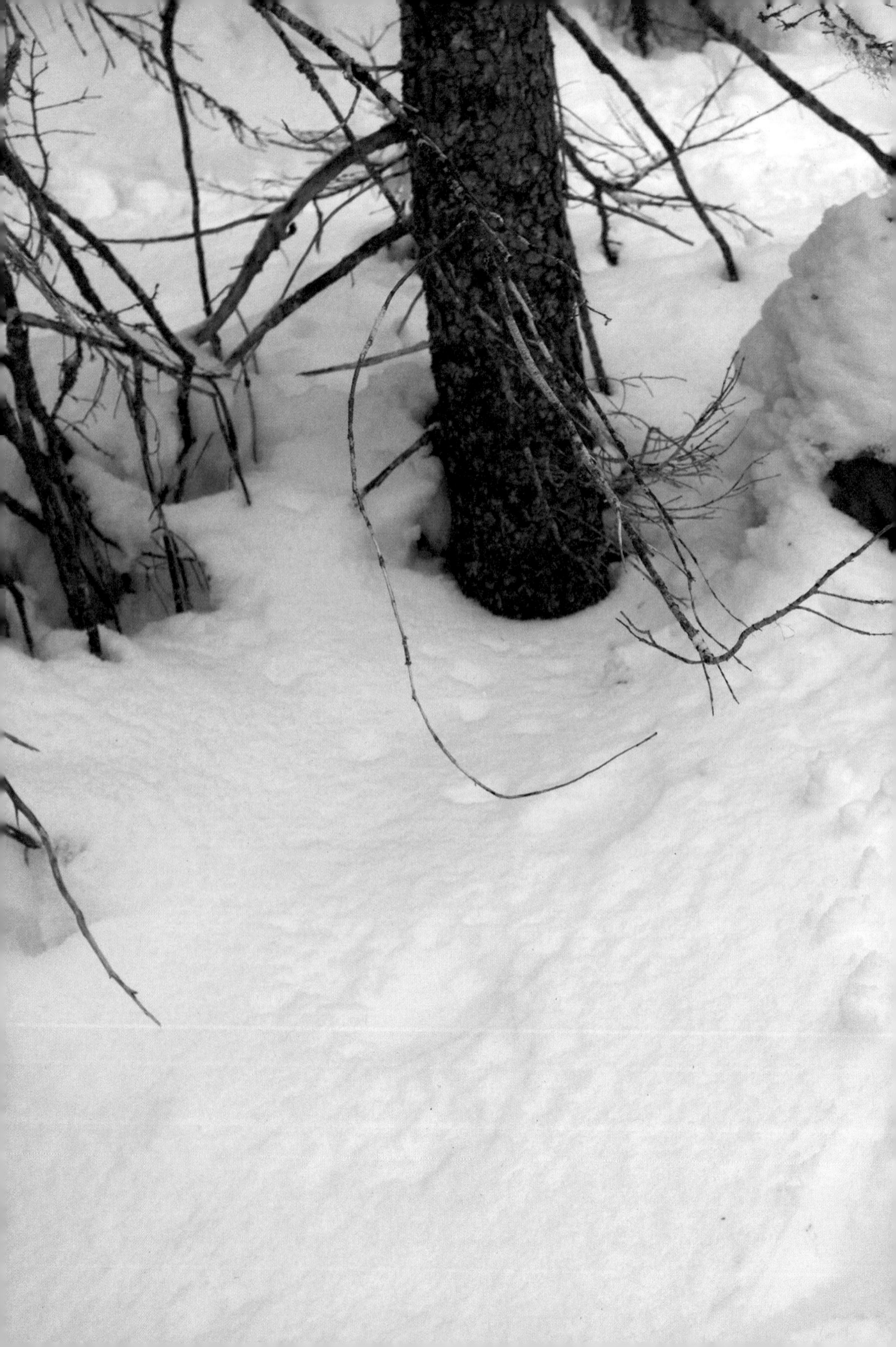

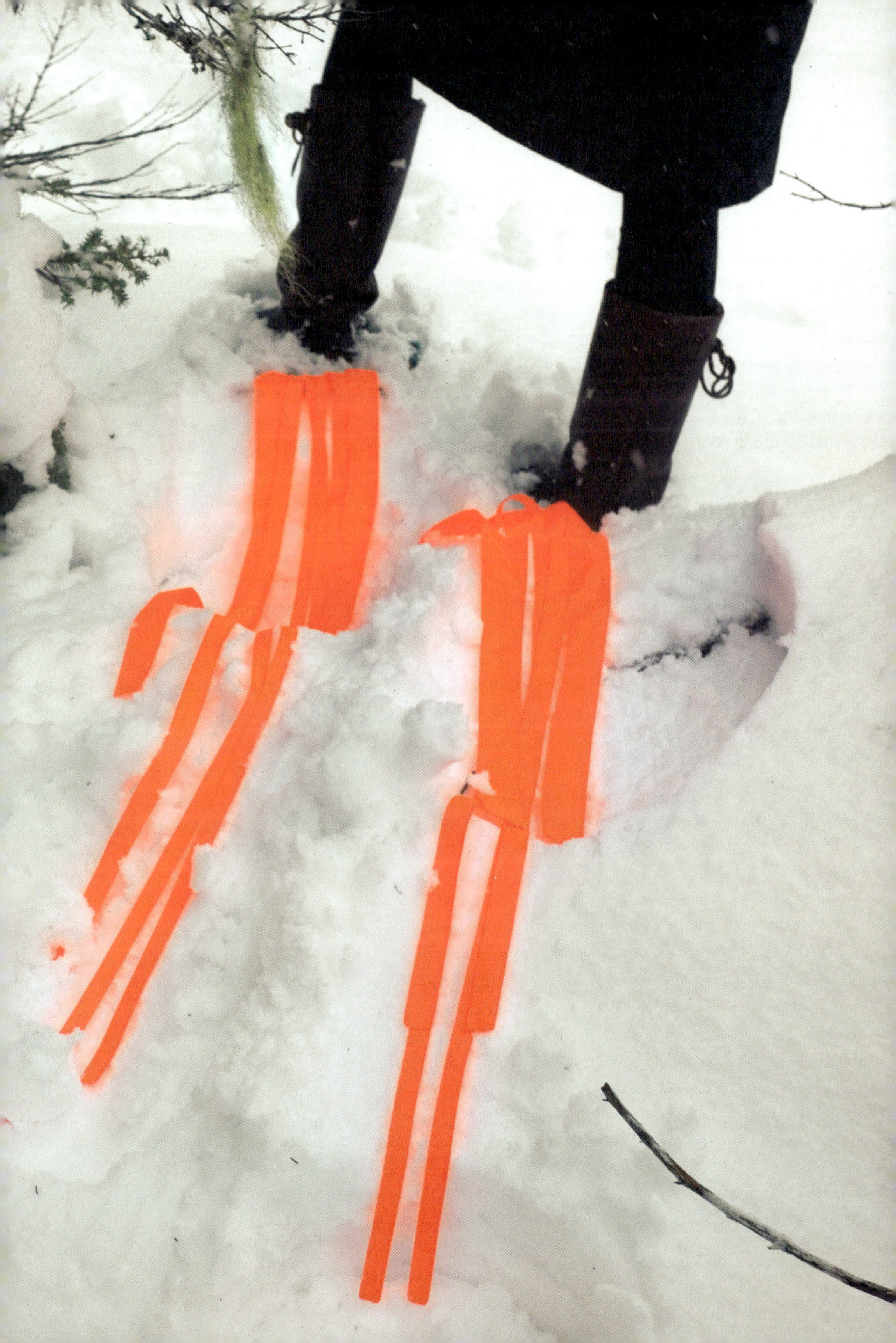

CANDICE HOPKINS

TO HEAR WHAT THE EELS SAY, FIRST LOOK INTO THE WATER: ON CHERYL L'HIRONDELLE'S *NIPAWIWIN AKIKODJIWAN: PIMIZI OHCI*

No matter what we are speaking about, whenever I have a conversation with Cheryl L'Hirondelle, the subject inevitably turns to animals. She provides updates on her cat, and me, my horses. These updates are always about our evolving relationships with them, what we have learned about them, what they are telling us, how we can be more attentive listeners. To set the record straight, the animals are never the ones being unclear, it's always us. It was not surprising when Cheryl began to describe a new project to me with a very different kind of collaborator—a group of freshwater eels, whose home is at the headwaters of Pipe Bowl Falls near Ottawa, Canada.

When she first conceived of her project, Cheryl wanted to do something in honor of former Chief Theresa Spence and Spence's hunger strike on the unceded territory of Victoria Island, to bring better health—at the very least, clean water and safe housing—to her people, clean water and adequate housing being promises in their treaties with the crown.[1] Spence's action, for the betterment of her home community, was concurrent with a national one—Idle No More, a Native resistance that spread through the veins of social media to Indian Reserves and shopping malls across so-called Canada. The group was formed as a means to call attention to the damage of omnibus bills that then Conservative government under former prime minister Harper was pushing through, which would have further eroded Native rights in Canada, including the Water Protections Act that has been upheld since 1882 by royal decree.[2] Suddenly, our voices were setting the temperature of discourse in the nation, and mainstream Canadians were

1 Spence had declared a formal state of emergency in her fly-in community of Attawapiskat First Nation in northern Ontario. Despite—or in-spite of—this desperate measure, those on Parliament Hill weren't paying attention. Getting them to do so meant that she had to take more drastic action and put her body and her own health on the line, days, turned to weeks of public starvation, to get those in positions of power on the hill to budge, even a little.

2 For more on Spence's action, please see the archive compiled by Aboriginal Peoples Television Network: https://www.aptnnews.ca/tag/attawapiskat-chief-theresa-spence/.

For more on Idle No More, including its founding and current actions, visit: https://idlenomore.ca/. Omnibus bills are unique to Canada. The term implies a bill that seeks to amend, repeal, or enact several acts within related but separate parts of the bill. The Harper government was strategically burying Acts within larger bills that were eroding Indigenous rights in Canada. The

learning about the dire living conditions on many reserves and how decades of government promises and legal obligations had done little to alleviate generational inequity and suffering, and in many cases, simply made it worse. These are the machinations of settler colonialism. In Canada, there is violence embedded in promises of “reconciliation” because it is always on the government’s terms and their timeline. It is never about making amends, it is always about placating, just enough so that we stop raising our voices, now and certainly then.

“teach-ins” that were part of the early Idle No More movement helped share this knowledge more broadly among Indigenous people, including lawyers and legal scholars.

Yet, beneath it all, quietly swimming around Victoria Island, were the eels. They have their own profound story to tell about ill health and population decline as well as shared tenacity and survivance despite the odds. They were—and are—similarly trying to catch the ear of those in power. You see, as they voiced to the artist, their kind is deeply impacted by the building of dams, which proliferated across Turtle Island like its own form of westward expansion, the kind propelled by the fervor of Manifest Destiny. This time, instead of a steam-powered train, expansion takes the form of banal infrastructure: earthen or concrete barriers that direct or restrict the natural course of water, affecting all the beings who depend on it. Because freshwater eels from all continents, save for Antarctica, spawn in one specific place on earth—known as the Sargasso Sea—at the age of twenty-five, the damming of rivers is dire to their species’ survival.

For *Nipawiwin Akikodjiwan: Pimizi ohci*, the eels weren’t relegated to simply being the subject, they were the collaborators. And like any good collaboration, this work was done with consent and mutual respect. At just over thirty-five minutes long, the immersive audio-visual installation becomes a textual and auditory declaration of every known translation for the word “eel.” This text scrolls like a slow ticker tape along the bottom of the projections.

Some of the voices sound inhuman, words clearly generated by computers that will always sound alien to our ears. Others are soft and lyrical; these ones voice the words that sound the most complex to English-speaking listeners—words in Indigenous languages. Cheryl shared that when she was working on the translations, she learned that words audiated in Indigenous languages via Google Translate were recordings of real human speakers, while common languages, including most western ones, were read by AI-generated voices.

The image and sound of falling water in the installation is of Akikodjiwan Falls, right next to Victoria Island. It is here where the eels climb a fish ladder, which inadvertently plays a role in determining their gender (those who later become female tend to the be ones who make it farther upstream, the males remain closer to the estuaries). Shortly after they hatch, eels are transparent, but with visible organs, which biologists refer to as the "glass eel" phase. Cheryl transposes images of the glass eels overtop the running falls. It is in this phase that they begin their more than a thousand-mile journey from their birthing grounds back to their home-waters. How each eel knows where to go is knowledge to which only they are privy.

The eels felt they were best represented in the installation in this beginning life phase, because our species tends to be more sympathetic to babies and the very young. From this state of sympathetic vulnerability, they are imploring us to pay attention. Dams, like the one that deeply impacts this group of eels, don't just damage visible ecosystems, they profoundly damage the ones within the water as well. Our insatiable need for power is not just harming our world, but their world, too. They are telling us this as clearly as they can. What we need to do is simple: heed their call.

GABRIELLE L'HIRONDELLE HILL

LEARNING FROM MATERIALS

p. 45
Gabrielle L'Hirondelle Hill, *X-tend*, 2021. Pantyhose, tobacco, thread, dried flowers, and rabbit fur. 12.5 × 10.8 × 13.5 inches (31.75 × 27.43 × 34.29 centimeters). Photo courtesy of the artist and Cooper Cole Gallery.

p. 46
Gabrielle L'Hirondelle Hill, *Purse*, 2019. Pantyhose, tobacco, dandelion, locket, bluebell, tobacco seeds, seed pod, horseshoe charm, thread, 6 × 5 × 5 inches (15.2 × 12.7 × 12.7 centimeters). Photo courtesy of the artist and Cooper Cole Gallery.

pp. 46–47
Gabrielle L'Hirondelle Hill, *Counterblaste*, 2021. Pantyhose, tobacco, beer can tabs, plastic flowers, dried flowers, earring beaded by Cheryl L'Hirondelle, thread, charms, running shoes, rabbit-fur earrings, nail polish. 9.5 × 79 × 26 inches (24.13 × 200.66 × 66.04 centimeters). Photo courtesy of the artist and Cooper Cole Gallery.

p. 47
Gabrielle L'Hirondelle Hill, *Spread*, 2021. Pantyhose, tobacco, thread, charms, and rabbit fur. 12.3 × 9.3 × 10.5 inches (31.24 × 23.62 × 26.67 centimeters). Photo courtesy of the artist and Cooper Cole Gallery.

First, these rabbits were made with tobacco, a plant that disperses outwards in all ways. Originating in the Peruvian Andes, tobacco had made its way to almost every corner of the Americas long before Europeans arrived. How did it move so far? Through trade, through exchange, through our ancestors' economic systems. I've read that prior to colonization, tobacco was so crucial to our social and economic practices that it was the number one item of exchange, the product moved most often and in the highest quantity through the trade routes across the continents.[1] Those systems survived capitalism, though I didn't recognize my own participation in them until recently.

My grandmother, Dorothe Stevenson, was a member of the Michel First Nation, and her father's people were from Papaschase. I'm part of the second generation of our family living away from our traditional lands, I'm mixed-race Cree and English and non-status. Yet, thinking about and working with tobacco as an artist taught me that when I put tobacco down, when I give it to someone, when I'm asking for a teaching, when I offer it, then I am taking part in that Cree and Metis ancestral economy. When I think about the difference between the act of paying for a teaching, or paying for food, and giving tobacco for those things, I learn a lot about what kind of alternative to capitalism Indigenous economies might offer. I also learn by talking and listening to my mother, Madeleine MacIvor, to Bernadette Spence, Bernadette's late husband Dave Pranteau, and to Tom McCallum.[2]

Secondly, these rabbits are a family. The large one, *Counterblaste*, is a mom, just like I became around the time I made her.[3]

1 Iain Gately, *Tobacco: A Cultural History of How an Exotic Plant Seduced Civilization* (New York: Grove, 2002).

2 Another great source is Rauna Kuokkanen, Research Professor of Arctic Indigenous Studies at the University of Lapland (Finland) and Adjunct Professor of Indigenous Studies and Political Science at the University of Toronto.

3 I named her after *A Counterblaste to Tobacco*, a treatise written by King James VI of Scotland and I of England in 1604 who expresses his disgust with tobacco as something that he connects to Indigenous bodies, Indigenous knowledge, Indigenous economies, Indigenous sexuality, and finally argues that tobacco poses a threat to English society and his kingdom.

She is roughly my size and is wearing my shoes. She has earrings and beads that were made and given to me by various friends, who are also artists: Cheryl L'Hirondelle, Tania Willard, Chandra Melting Tallow, and Jane Harms. I was thinking about how along with the violent, ongoing transition from our economies to capitalism here, there is also a transition in family structure, sexuality, the role of women, the conception of gender, etc. At the same time, some kinds of motherhood or parenthood remain somehow incompatible with capitalism. This experience of parenthood becomes a source of resistance. So maybe this work is my way of linking those two ideas that I've been thinking about—Indigenous economies and reproductive labor, families, caretaking—as both potential threats to capitalism and models of other possibilities.

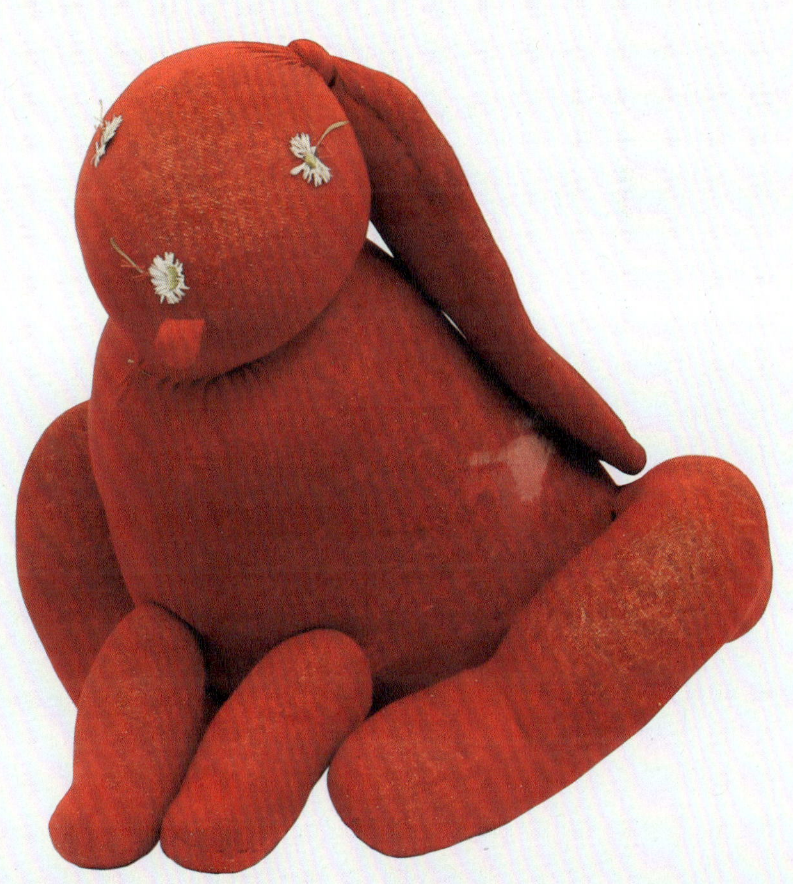

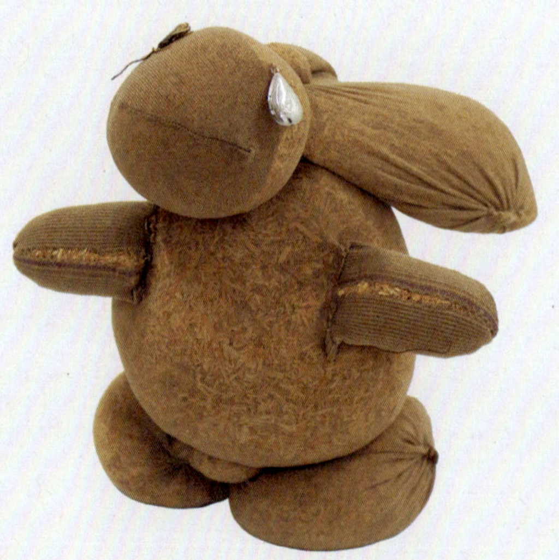

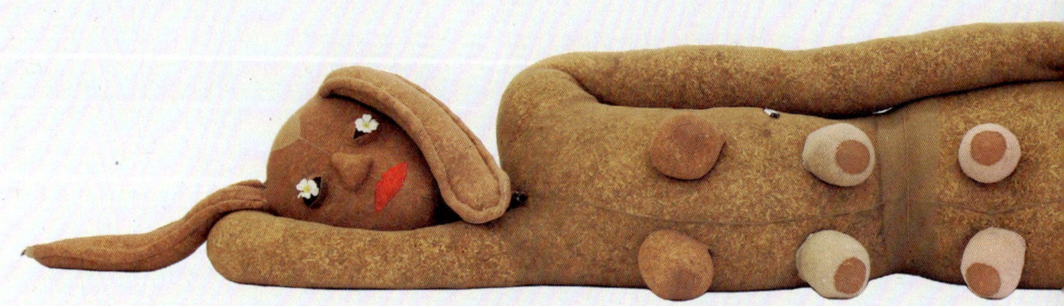

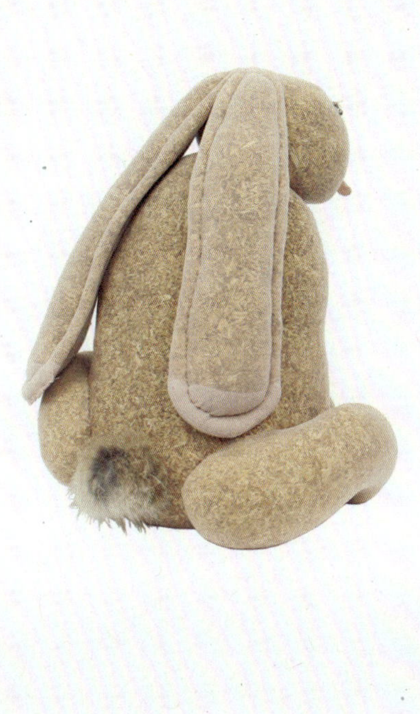

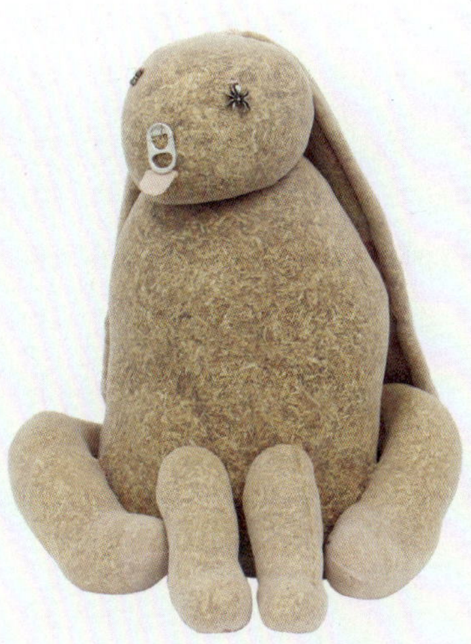

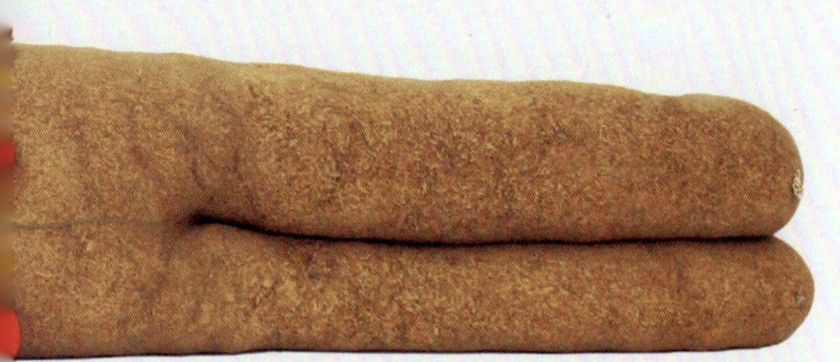

RAVEN DAVIS

MY MOTHER GAVE ME MY IMFA—INDIGENOUS MASTER'S OF FINE ARTS

My mother, a beautiful Anishinaabe woman from Manitoba, taught me how to paint when I was five years old. She was kind and patient and once in a while would even let me paint at her desk. Those moments were the safest I ever felt with her. When she sat down to make something, I knew she would be in a good mood for at least a couple of hours. I knew she wouldn't be thinking about how to feed me and my brother our next meal, how much laundry needed to be done, what bills needed to be paid or whether or not my father would show up for his biweekly visit.

I remember the specific way she laid out her art supplies—paints lined up from darkest to lightest, brushes drying tips-up in a soup can, a T-square aligned with the metal edge of her homemade drafting table and a few secondhand books about color, design, and architecture. I thought my mom was the smartest, coolest, and best artist in the whole wide world. I thought I was living with someone famous who should be on TV or something. When I would watch my mom paint, I would sit as still as a deer in headlights. My eyes were wide open, my ears cocked; I could hear the sound of every brushstroke and every time she'd hold her breath to make a straight line. I knew when I grew up, I wanted to be just like her.

I don't remember people asking me what I wanted to be when I got older. At least not at the age where I'd be old enough to truly grasp the question. Nor did anyone ask me what I was going to do after high school; instead, they questioned if I'd even achieve my grade twelve. It wasn't until I was much older that I realized I could earn money through art. When I finally stated that I wanted to be an artist, people would always discourage me with the adage "every artist is a starving artist." I always wondered why someone would want to do something that would cause them to suffer. Now I know why. I've learned that you don’t have to suffer for the things you love; it’s about reassessing what matters to you, what you want to prioritize, and what you’re willing to let go of.

I never thought about how much money artists made, but I knew that making art made my mother’s tears go away. I knew art was something priceless. I learned that we had access to happiness and didn’t have to pay for it. I knew that whatever she made, it made our apartment beautiful. Even the way she’d hang her work in the hallway made me feel rich. I felt like when my friends came over they’d think we were *rolling in it*, even though the work was mostly hung with thumbtacks and tape.

In the very back of her supply shelf, there was a bottle that stood out—it was taller than the others and had the most beautifully printed paper label. The bottle was labeled “Indian ink” and I thought for sure it had to have been made in Manitoba. I thought “Indian ink” was only used by Indians. I used to think that when I used it, I made art that held some kind of ancestral magic. Like it didn’t matter what I created with it; it would turn out to be beautiful and truthful. As if art could lie.

When my mom painted, she would set out paper for me and would give me a few of her brushes, but not the “good ones”—those were reserved for special days. She used them infrequently, and cherished whatever was made with them. I was convinced they were made with the softest, whitest unicorn hair. I used to believe that when I grew up, my mom would eventually let me use the unicorn brushes, once I could prove to her I was good enough. It was only then that I would make art that would sing and dance right off the canvas. She used to keep these special brushes separate from all the rest and cleaned them with the same care and gentleness that she used when she washed my hair. I knew that when those brushes came out, my mom meant business, and whatever she was about to make would be breathtaking. On the weekends when my mother wasn't working, she would take us for drives in the country. She'd pack a few sandwiches, fill up the thermos and we'd be off. While exploring the back roads of Caledon and going off the beaten trails in Algonquin Park, my mom would gather materials that she thought were interesting to paint on or make something out of. In this, she taught me that the earth provides materials for us to make beautiful things. I began to understand at a very young age how much we depend on the land, how we must protect it so it can continue to care for us. And I understood that the earth made its own art, and that adults have names for the works, such as "sunsets," "northern lights," "moss," "rivers and rain."

My mother taught me to always source and gather different materials to make art with. She would always experiment and never settle on one medium. In my eyes, my mother was art—the absolutely longest duration performance, she would fill any room she entered. She was light, contrast, shape and depth, and held stories that would baffle even the best curatorial writers and academics. Her skin glowed golden-brown and her hands transformed and became a duplicate of every tool ever made; she made everything we couldn't afford. Her passion to create was inspiring. She carefully balanced life and her children and made time when she could to take part-time night courses that helped her escape the fists of my father.

My mother would sit me down and explain her brushes, and the choice of paint or clay she was using, and she was the first to inspire me to fall in love with drafting, typography, and architecture. My mother taught me everything I know about art. She was my school. She gave me my degree and my IMFA—my very own Indigenous Master's of Fine Arts.

TJ CUTHAND

13 EGGS

13 Eggs follows filmmaker and artist TJ Cuthand's journey through the physical, emotional, and bureaucratic processes of in vitro fertilization, the subject of a documentary in progress. Through intimate storytelling, he details the nuances of this experience as a trans person, questioning his own motivations for this undertaking while connecting them with our collective biological needs to hold and be held. *13 Eggs* battles hope, fear, failure, dysmorphia, loneliness, and uncertainty. In this open letter, addressed directly to his eggs, Cuthand recollects his various trials, which were ultimately unsuccessful. As a timestamp that records a particular moment in his process of documenting loss, Cuthand's letter subtly reveals the intersections of Indigeneity, queer love, and family.

pp. 58–59
TJ Cuthand, stills from *13 Eggs*, 2022, video, 14 minutes. Photos courtesy of the artist.

Dear Eggs,

Hi. I know you'll be gone by the time people read this. And by the time people see my video about trying to make a baby with you. I find it so cool that you bring half the genes into the equation. But it didn't work out. And I'd talked about doing this as it was happening, so it wasn't, like, a secret attempt at making an embryo, everyone on my Facebook knew what I was going through.

I think making a documentary about my body's process going through partial in vitro fertilization was more ambitious than I expected. There are so many feelings around failure connected to it. And I was already disadvantaged because my uterus doesn't work. So, it's not like babymaking could be a quiet, casual exchange of semen in a cup or something among friends. It involved a fertility clinic, where all the rules around donor sperm were complicated, so we pretended to be a couple in the clinic. We looked so obviously UNLIKE a straight couple though.

But even in the beginning, just getting the eggs retrieved showed me how difficult this was to do alone. There was a group that met at that clinic—single-by-choice parents who could talk about making babies alone. I never went. I don't know why. Maybe because I wanted a partner to show up for me, even though no one serious ever had before.

This film is about failure. My failure to make a baby, my failure to find a long-term romantic partner. We are always supposed to seek out happy endings, but sometimes the endings are really just, "well, that happened."

I didn't get to freeze embryos because the fertilized cells just stopped dividing. You, Eggs, were just not enough. And it cost so much money, but I had to be sure, right? I just didn't want to totally give up.

This process took years. One year for egg retrieval. A couple of years later, trying to fertilize with my friend's sperm. And then just sitting with the answer, that my fertility journey had reached an end, and trying to figure out how to finish telling a story like that.

Because I always want to give people hope, right? No one wants to hear that someone tried to have kids and it didn't work out; that could mean that when they try to have kids, it won't work out. It's like facing a kind of mortality.

Trying to talk about my body as a reproducing body was also extremely dysphoric for me as a trans person. I've never really thought much about having dysphoria in my body; I was always happy with what I had even though I was seeing myself as a more masculine/butch/boy figure. But going to the clinic every other day meant getting trans vaginal ultrasounds, blood work, needles, pain. I never really liked the trans vaginal ultrasounds; it just required so much attention to an area that usually is very sexy in a not very sexy way. It made me feel like all that mattered was what my ovaries were doing, and in a way it was true. I was just supposed to be growing follicles. But spreading my legs for ultrasound techs every other day for two weeks, that was A LOT.

I did get a strange needle kink, though, from having to give myself fertility shots every morning. I didn't really explore it much after that. But following the first three or four needles, I started getting into the routine. Mixing medications, drawing it all into a syringe, finding a place to poke. It was comforting. Even though the injection spots were sore for days, and my body built up sorenesses as each day brought another shot, there was something about doing it that made me feel alive.

There was something sad about it, too. I was always really conscious that I was self-administering these shots. Because for other couples at the fertility clinic, their partners were administering these shots. They were doing it together. And I was doing it alone. I was seeing the doctor alone, until my friend and I had to fake being a couple later on. But ultimately, I would have been raising this baby alone.

Time passed and now my only chance at parenthood is to adopt a baby. But life stopped me again, because suddenly things were different. The pandemic was happening. Climate change was accelerating. And I wasn't ready to parent anymore. I know if I'd had a kid by then, I would have kept being a parent. But I didn't have a kid, and things changed.

Being a performance artist, I wanted to try and bring eggs as a symbol into this video. I used thirteen eggs, the number that had been retrieved from my ovaries, and sat cradling them in my lap. It felt precarious as I performed this, conscious of the fragility and weight of each raw egg I held. Then my friend Vanessa Dion Fletcher took those eggs and threw them at my crotch. We learned that a raw egg thrown at a naked body will just bounce off. But if you give them a preemptive crack on the floor, you can get a good splatter.

I also put eggs in my freezer. I had a whole vision of what a frozen egg would be like, but even twenty-four hours later it wasn't frozen. I had a stop-motion animation of an egg disintegrating as the shell is pulled away from it. I put eggs in my flower garden.

An egg is a very elegant shape. And so versatile. They make great breakfasts. And shakshuka is amazing. And huevos rancheros is probably my all-time favorite egg dish. I had really good huevos rancheros in New York City just a few blocks from Times Square. But

I don't remember where. I wish I could find it again. I know they used green salsa for it. It was majestic.

When I was in art school, one of my assigned projects was to make a site-specific installation. So I took parts of my diary and wrote them onto large paper tags, and tied them to smashed eggshells that I had hot-glue-gunned back together. I left them around downtown Vancouver. It was my first experience putting personal details, directly from my diary, into the public sphere. It probably started a bad habit that I carried on into life and art and social media, where I say some things too openly. People often carry these stories in secrecy.

Especially stories about trying to conceive. No one wants to grieve a loss like that publicly. It's something for your best friend or your mom. Or your partner, if you have one.

Eggs, I think I still have some of you inside me. I don't know for sure though, and I'm not going to check. I haven't had a period since 2014. Menopause is looming now, and since I don't have a period anyway, I don't know what my hormones are doing at any particular time. If I did have a period, I would at least be able to notice its absence, or its changing behavior. But I don't, so I'm lost in this phase of my life.

The last person I really liked was a year younger than me, and when the topic of children was brought up, they said they were too old for them now anyway. I suppose that was true for them. It made me wonder if it was true for me, if there really is an age when I shouldn't think about having children anymore.

I don't know the purpose of making this film, I don't want people to feel bad for me. I paid $20,000 to find out if I could have kids and the end result is no, I can't. I got to have eggs smashed on me while I processed this loss. I got to wonder about fertility as a trans masculine person and what that means for me. And I struggled with feelings of inadequacy about having a uterus that I had voluntarily made barren before deciding to try to have kids.

Eggs, you are both long gone and still here. You tried and you also exist in blissful unfertilized states in my body. Eggs, I'm glad I was able to try something, even when it failed.

TJ Cuthand
April 8, 2022

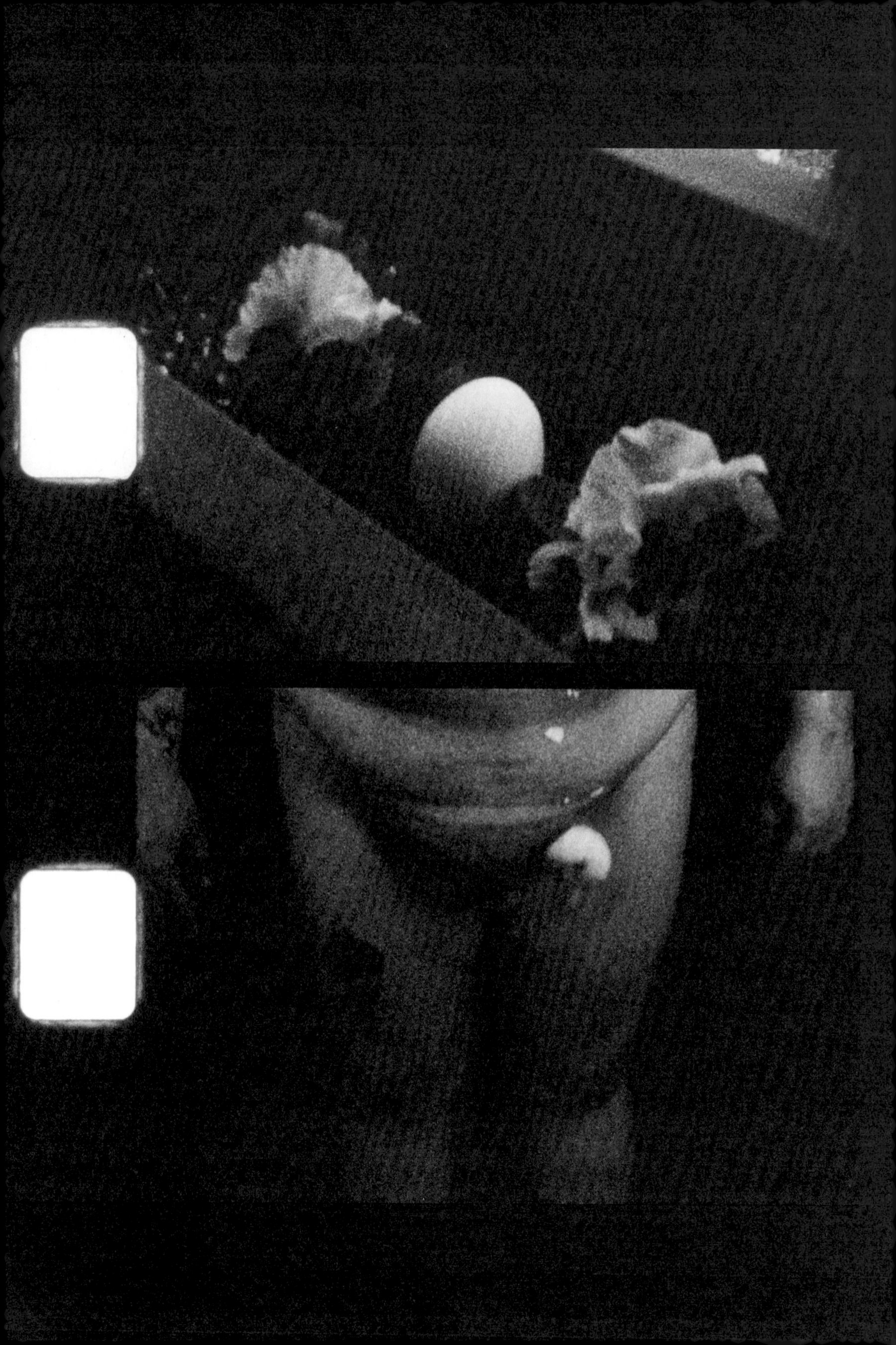

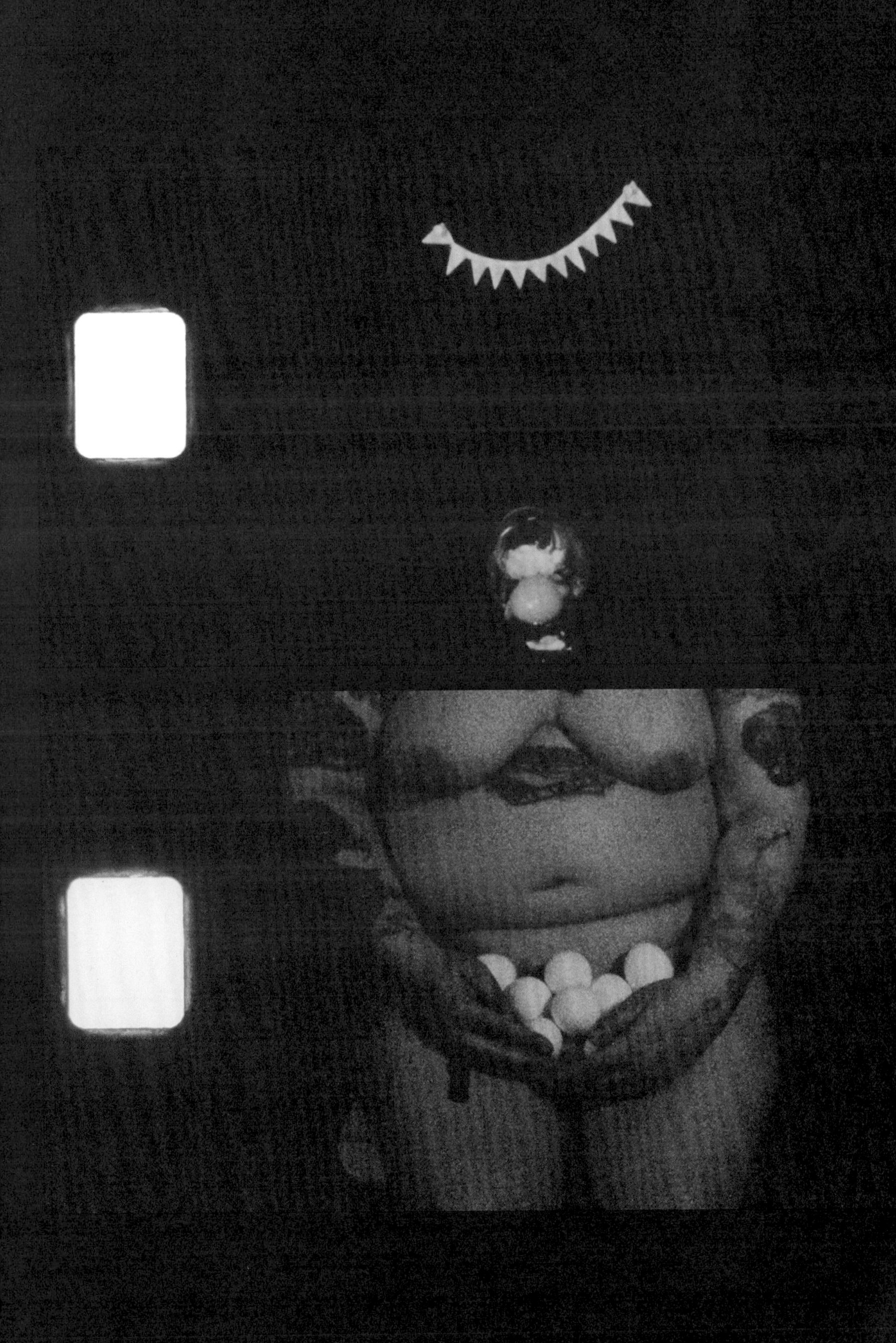

VANESSA DION FLETCHER

I WANT PINK DRIP

Vanessa Dion Fletcher's artistic practice explores representations of biological processes, utilizing media ranging from porcupine quills to menstrual blood to evoke the visual signifiers of what defines a body both socially and politically. Dion Fletcher's performance *I Want Pink Drip* contrasts the notion of the anthropological and medical body by creating space for the artist's own definitions. The imagery of dripping and staining shares a close visual proximity to menstruation, illustrating that our bodies are fluid rather than rigid or fixed. Her work evokes the symbolic power of materials as she uses dye from hibiscus, blueberry, and onion plants to connect the external human body to the internal plant body.

pp. 61–62
Vanessa Dion Fletcher, *I Want Pink Drip*, 2022. Performance. Photos courtesy of the artist.

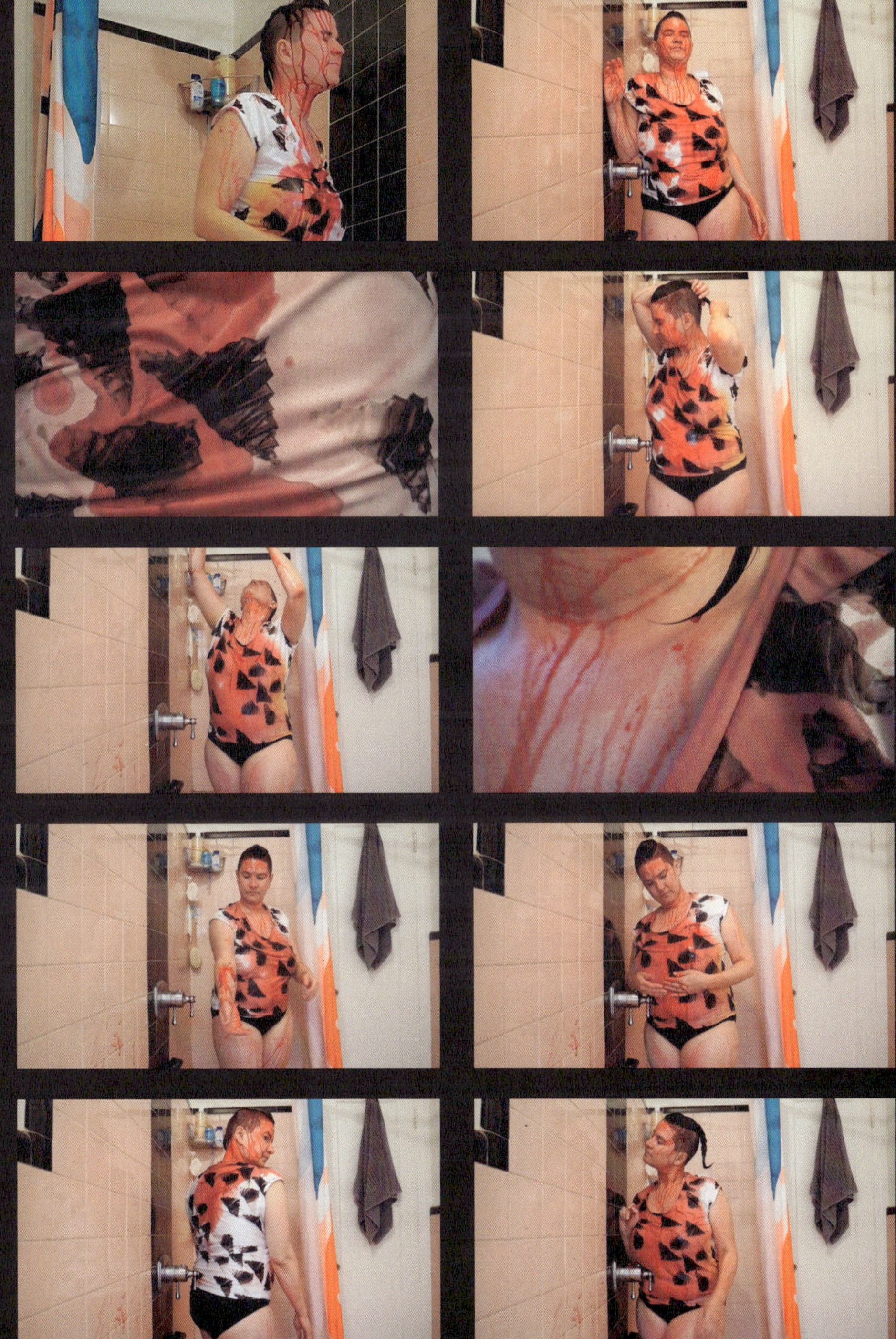

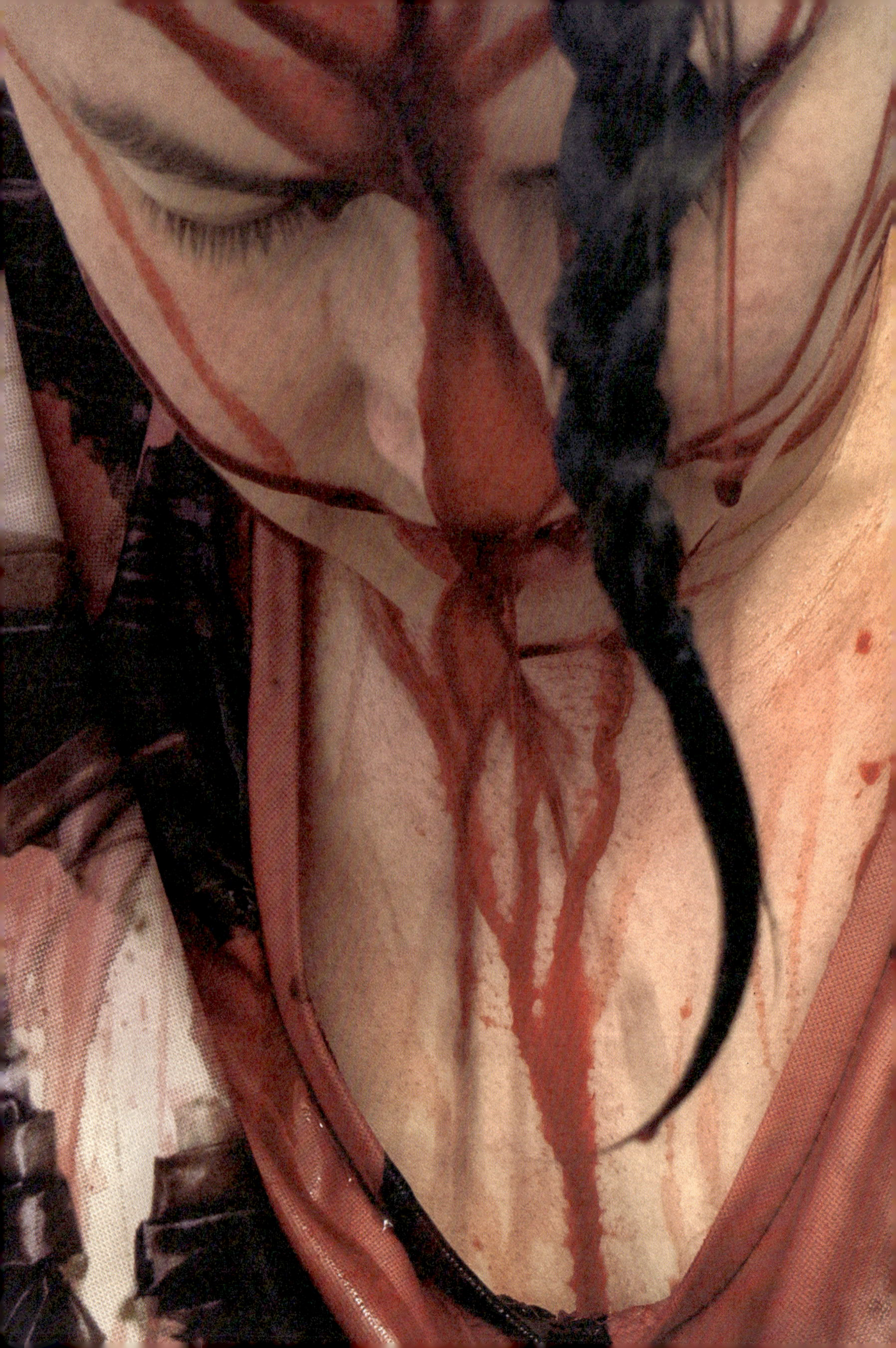

amniotic
aqueous humor
bile
blood plasma
milk
cerebrospinal
cerumen
chyle
exudates
gastric juice
lymph
mucus
pericardial
peritoneal
pleural
pus
saliva
sebum
serous
semen
sputum
synovial
sweat
tears
urine
vomit

SKEENA REECE

VICTIMPRINCESSMOTHER

Through humor, improvisation, and disguise, Skeena Reece takes on multifaceted personas to address somber realities. With her recurring TikTok persona Victimprincessmother, Reece parodies and interrogates stereotypes and expectations that surround Indigenous women. Using filters and sounds to distort her likeness and voice, Victimprincessmother's otherworldly appearance intentionally, provocatively, unsettles viewers, confronting them with their own assumptions about what Indigenous women should look and sound like, as well as what spaces they are allowed to occupy. Evoking the Hopi "sacred clown" or the trickster, the satirical videos embody the art of misdirection, discussing ongoing political grievances of performative action, lack of representation in the media, food sovereignty, and land back. Reece effectively turns the physical and the digital space into sites of reflection.

pp. 65–67
Skeena Reece, *Mother and Child*, 2021. Kodak Portra 800. Photos courtesy of the artist.

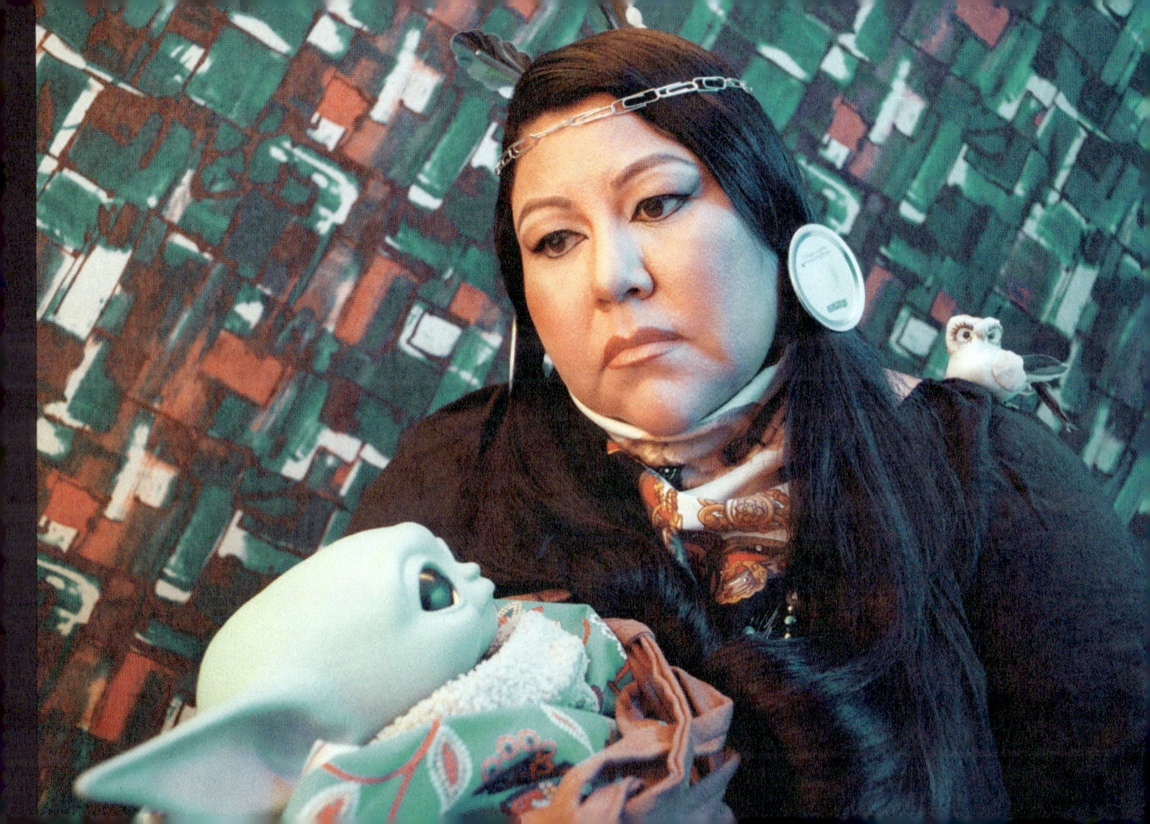

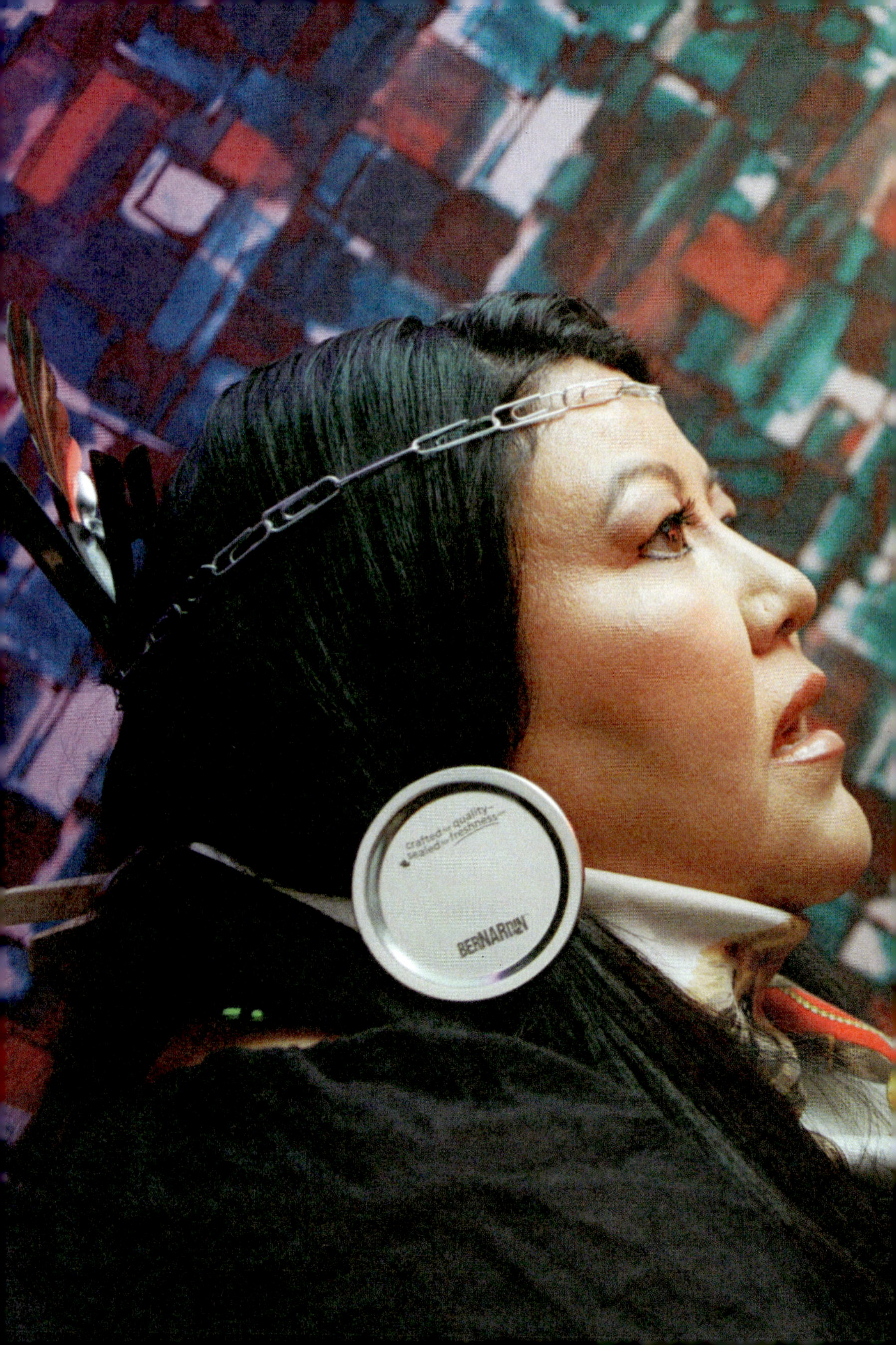
crafted for quality
sealed for freshness
BERNARDIN

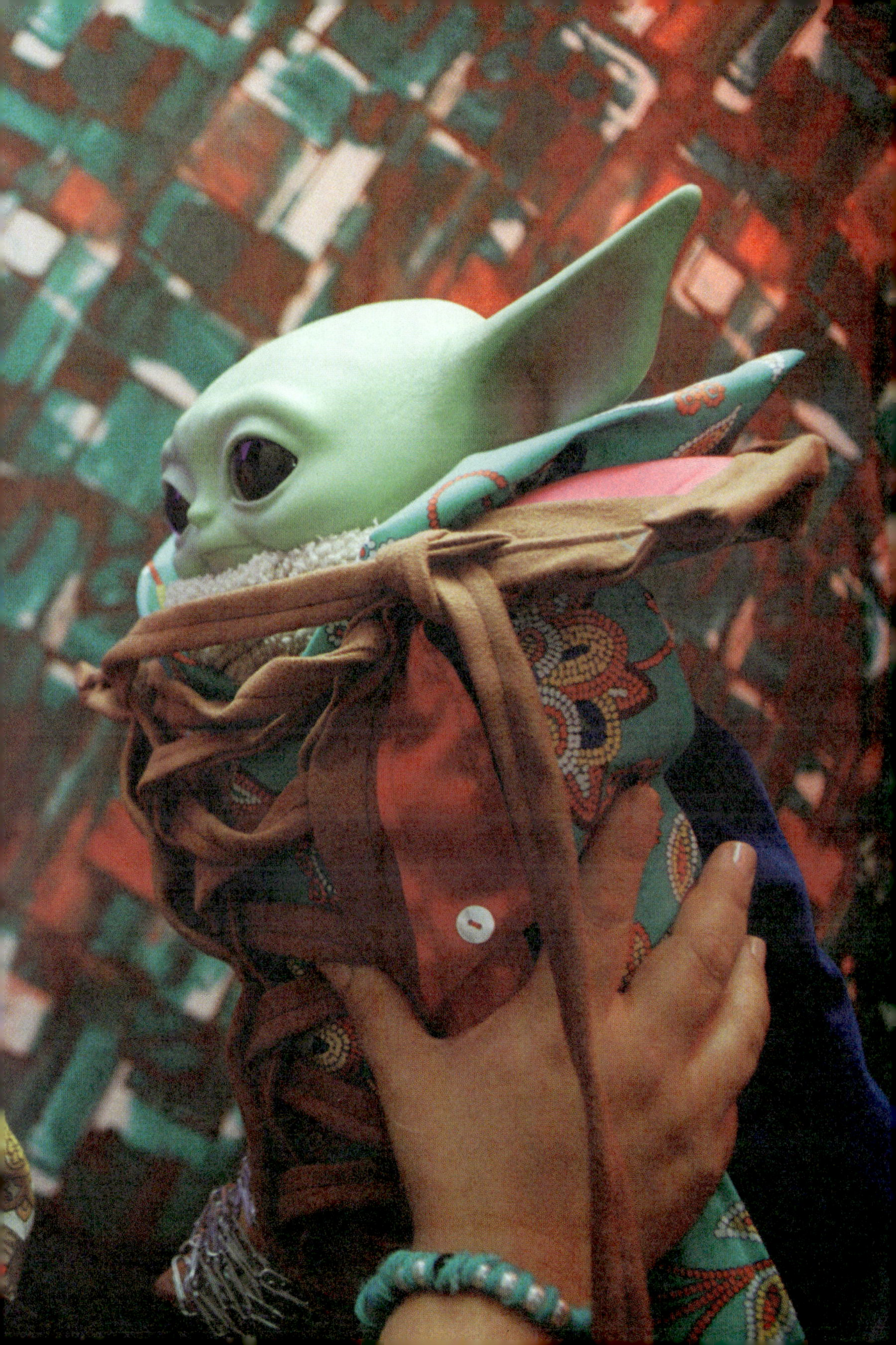

GEORGIANA UHLYARIK

HER WORKING HANDS: ON LAAKKULUK WILLIAMSON BATHORY

p. 73
Installation view, *Inuit Art in Motion*, co-curated by Laakkuluk Williamson Bathory and Anna Hudson, Fudger Rotunda, Art Gallery of Ontario, Toronto, November 24, 2004–January 9, 2005. Photo © AGO; courtesy of the artist.

Laakkuluk Williamson Bathory, *IIitarivingaa? Do You Recognize Me?*, public opening, Art Gallery of Ontario, Toronto, Ontario, August 7–October 30, 2004. Photo © AGO; courtesy of the artist.

Laakkuluk Williamson Bathory and Mary Pitsiulak, *Tunirrusiangit*, public opening, Art Gallery of Ontario, June 2018. Photo © AGO; courtesy of the artist.

"I want the installation to hold you." This is what Laakkuluk tells me when we first start talking about installing her work in amidst Inuit carvings gathered by her parents. She wants to surround you with the sound of her throat singing, laughing, crying, and speaking with her friend Celina Kalluk—two Inuit women, mothers, artists, daughters, standing across from each other five years ago in their now home base of Iqaluit, Nunavut. She wants to draw you into *silaup putunga*—the porthole into the universe—through her pupil, into the expanse of *sila*—the all-powerful Inuktitut word that encompasses the universe, the environment and the intellect.[1] Laakkuluk Williamson Bathory wants you to imagine what it means to hold, carry, and turn in your palms small, transforming figures carved out of gray stone by the knowing, working hands of Kivalliq sculptors, lifelong friends of her parents.[2]

In her most recent multimedia installation *Naak silavit qeqqa?*, Laakkuluk activates all our senses to consider her familial question, "Where is the middle of your sila?"[3] Her collaborative work, Silaup Putunga, 2018, is a double-sided projection on a large translucent framed screen that hangs diagonally from the ceiling in the center of the octagonal neoclassical gallery space on the first floor of the Art Gallery of Ontario (AGO).[4] It is an ever-changing sequence of moving images—seeping into each other through the screen—creating an evolving narrative, evoking a "living" print—her honoring of generations of Inuit artists who created a compelling vision of the Inuit worldview with pencils, stencils, and markers on paper.

1 For an expanded discussion see: Laakkuluk Williamson Bathory and Georgiana Uhlyarik, "Silaup Putunga in Context," in *Qummut Qukiria! Art, Culture, and Sovereignty Across Inuit Nunaat and Sápmi: Mobilizing the Circumpolar North* (Fredricton, NB: Goose Lane Editions, 2022), 140–47; or watch "Art in the Spotlight: Laakkuluk Williamson Bathory." June 23, 2020. https://www.youtube.com/watch?v=Rda4mHoMTAs.

2 Born 1979, Kalaalleq-Greenlandic Inuk.

3 Laakkuluk's mother, Karla Jessen Williamson, asked her this when she was young, just as she had been asked by her aunts, and now she asks her grandchildren. There is no right answer, she says, and how you answer or where you point changes over time.

4 Laakkuluk Williamson Bathory and Jamie Griffiths's *Silaup Putunga*, 2018, was commissioned by Anna Hudson and me for the Mobilizing Inuit Cultural Heritage and the Art Gallery of Ontario as part of *Tunirrusiangit: Kenojuak Ashevak and Tim Pitsiulak* exhibition at the AGO (June 16–August 12, 2018). It was then acquired by AGO. Soundscape by Celina

Kalluk and Laakkuluk. AGO Purchase, with funds from the Joan Chalmers Inuit Art Fund, 2019. 2019/2324.

It is not the first time Laakkuluk brought motion and emotion to this very space and to Inuit art and artists. In 2004, she installed *Inuit Art in Motion*, an installation of stone and bone carvings of drumming and dancing bears, hunters, mothers, and other beings. There were several on a platform in the center, accompanied by a video projection of an Inuk drummer performing in AGO's atrium only a few spaces away.[5] This is when I first met her, and soon after understood her as a powerful performer in all aspects of her projects: in her writing, curating, advocacy, and, of course, in her film, theater, and visual work. I was reminded of her gathering of dancing and drumming beings decades later, in 2021, when we met in Ottawa for the unveiling of her Sobey award commissioned work *Nannuppugut! (We shot a bear!)*. Laakkuluk projected a video of herself drumming onto the hide of the nanoq that she shot when the she-bear stood up and leaned into the window of the family's cabin in August 2020.[6] Celebrating the spirit of her *nanoq* and the privilege of the encounter, Laakkuluk made herself an outfit honoring the color of the bear's flesh and drummed with nanoq's skull beside her.

In *Silaup Putunga*, Laakkuluk livens the screen by performing *uaajeerneq*, a Kalaallit (Greenlandic) mask dance—covering her face in black grease and drawing on it by scraping with her nails, adding red grease sometimes, and inserting wooden balls into her cheeks. It was first taught to her by her mother, Karla Jessen Williamson, and then she studied it with practitioners and the original recreators of *uaajeerneq* from the 1970s Kalaallit folk movement.[7] "[T]he purpose of doing the mask dancing is to unsettle people, to push their

5 *Inuit Art in Motion*, Fudger Rotunda, Art Gallery of Ontario, co-curated with Anna Hudson, November 27, 2004–January 9, 2005. https://ago.ca/exhibitions/inuit-art-motion. Accessed September 1, 2022.

6 Laakkuluk Williamson Bathory, "Nannuppugut!" in *Qummut Qukiria! Art, Culture, and Sovereignty Across Inuit Nunaat and Sápmi: Mobilizing the Circumpolar North* (Fredricton, NB: Goose Lane Editions, 2022) 100–13.

7 "Q & A with Laakkuluk Williamson Bathory," https://chancentre.com/news/q-a-with-laakkuluk.

boundaries, to see where fear exists, and what the limits of your sense of humor is. And to do a joyful and affirming celebration of sexuality."[8]

Filmed over several days at her family cabin, twenty-three kilometers southeast of Iqaluit (the one to be visited by the nanoq two years later), Laakkuluk slowly leads viewers through the Arctic landscape, as she chops ice, drives a Ski-Doo, aims a gun and shoots, cooks, walks through unbroken snow, and, with an ever-present raven above, performs. "What we wanted to create was a study of intimacy within a great expanse, … how tiny a human being I am within the vastness of the ice, and the ability to turn from a human into a semi-human or supernatural or unnatural creature, that *Uaajeerneq* is being able to rip through these realms, like piercing through something, piercing through an eyeball, piercing through the air, piercing into the ice. … Each emotion that comes out of the sound hits the imagery in a different way, so you can feel differently about each thing that you see."[9] Her performances are live and alive, and rupture any normative predictability to overcome discomfort, fear and limitations, seeking equanimity, resolve.[10] Equanimity is a word Laakkuluk taught me the meaning of, having known it but not ever understanding it as a sense and state of being until she pronounced it.

On the walls to the left and right of *Silaup Putunga* hang two small semicircular cases; their back panels are mirrored so that the small carvings are visible in the round. There is a man carrying a caribou, two throat singers holding and facing each other, a dog, a bird, a mother carrying her child in her amautik, and other shape-shifting beings, greeting each other. More importantly, the reflecting panels

8 Quoted in "Layers of Expression," AGO Insider, August 17, 2022, https://ago.ca/agoinsider/layers-expression.

9 "Silaup Putunga in Context," 144.

10 Laakkuluk has co-created and performed uaajeerneq in many productions, including, *Kiinalik: These Sharp Tools*, 2017, and *Ikumagialiit* ᐃᑯᒪᒋᐊᓖᑦ *(those that need fire)*, 2019, as well as in art museums, such as performances accompanying *Ilitarivingaa? Do You Recognize me?* at the AGO in Fall 2004. See https://laakkuluk.com/projects/ and https://ago.ca/exhibitions/ilitarivingaa-do-you-recognize-me.

expand the space by folding the outside in, completing the circular space beyond the limits of the wall, so that we as viewers are implicated inextricably. Our scale deceives us, becomes irrelevant, as we are transported through the porthole and we are held by the spirited carvings in their transformative space.

Laakkuluk's intelligent hands have held these carved beings growing up in her home, until they came to join the Inuit art collection at the AGO in 1989. A few years back, Laakkuluk brought her husband and three children into the vault to visit them, most especially, *Somersaulting Man* (1964), a dynamic being in mid-rounded spring.[11] He can be placed in so many different ways; he is in ever-constant motion. Laakkuluk's children cling to her the way children do no matter how grown up they are—they rub and lean and press against their mother when too much world is too near, and together in their hands they hold the carvings and each other. Whispering in Inuktitut, everyone is there with them, surrounding, embracing them, and I am witness because I have a badge that opens the locked door, the door behind which they are all kept until they are visited to hold and be held.

11 John Kavik (born Uqsuqtuuq, Nunavut, Canada, 1897, died Yellowknife, Northwest Territories, Canada, 1993), *Somersaulting Man: As I Think of Myself*, 1964, dark grey stone, 16.5 x 10.5 x 8.4 cm, AGO, Gift of Dr. Robert G. Williamson, C.M., 1989, 89/237.

Laakkuluk's working hands speak and feed. They are covered in seal fat, grease, gutting, beading, tending the *qulliq* so the light does not go out. They are laughing hands, storytelling hands, wiping beads of sweat from just that space of folds between her nose and mouth; they are hands crawling on the earth-cover in the summer, in the winter, out of seawater, in the snow; picking berries, they are fishing hands, birthing hands, hands with a drum, hands with a rifle, hands that killed a nanoq and are now marked by *tunniit* of parallel lines across the back of her hands "to celebrate this new state of being."[12] Inviting hands, she wants you to be held.

12 "Nannuppugut!" 111.

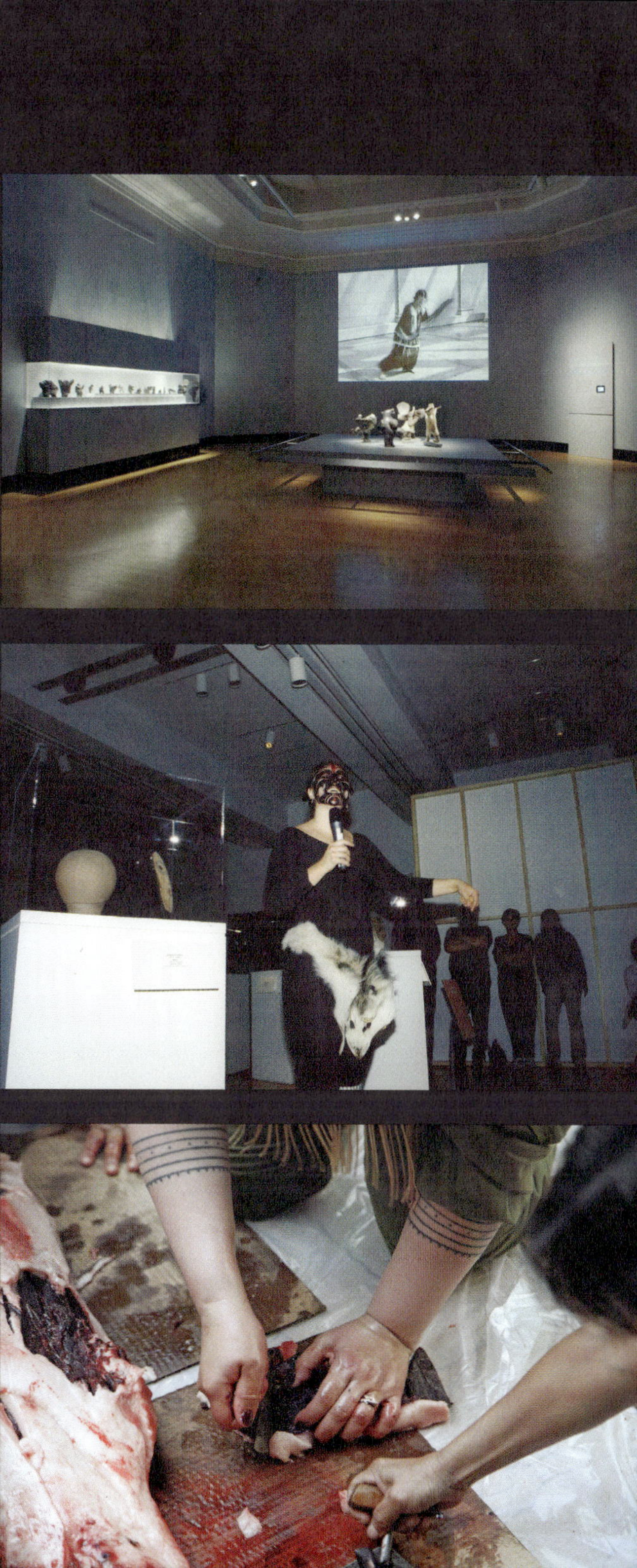

CATHY MATTES

WITNESSER: ON LORI BLONDEAU

pp. 78–79
Lori Blondeau (Cree/Saulteaux/Métis), *Witnesser*, with Theo Sims (British), August 26, 2022, WAG-Qaumajuq. Performance documentation, 15:15 minutes. Performance contributions by Jaimie Isaac, Melissa St. Goddard, and Grandfather Rocks. With assistance by Tamara Dolan, Curator, Senate of Canada, Heritage and Curatorial Services; Senator Patricia Bovey; Meg Diamond; Jenelle Tougas; and Shaneela Boodoo. Photos courtesy of the artist.

For the exhibition *Kwaata-nihtaawakihk*, held at the Winnipeg Art Gallery from March 18 to September 3, 2022, performance artist and educator Lori Blondeau and mixed-media artist Theo Sims collaborated to create an installation that addressed and stimulated reconciliation. Named after the Southern Michif words for "hard birth" and co-curated by Sherry Farrell Racette and myself, the exhibition commemorated the role of lii Michif in birthing the Province of Manitoba in 1870. It featured key documents, historic objects, and artwork from the past interwoven with contemporary art created by Michif, First Nations, and non-Indigenous artists. This included photographs, beadwork, film, painting, textiles, installation, sculpture, and, for the closing, a performance by Blondeau.

In the early stages of their collaboration, Blondeau encouraged Sims to look within himself and reflect upon his connection to this land, which led him to research power symbols from England that are embedded in the colonial fabric of Canada. He uncovered that in the late 1870s, during the early phases of the Canadian Confederation, judges in the Canadian Senate opted for the use of a Woolsack—a large, wool-stuffed cushion with a symbolic connection to the British Empire. Beginning in the 1300s, top judges and the Speaker of the House of Lords in the British Parliament sat together on a Woolsack when the reigning monarch delivered speeches. Sims and Blondeau borrowed the original Woolsack that was used in the Canadian Parliament until 1949 and incorporated it in their installation. In an effort to deepen his understanding and to further reconcile Canada's legacy of colonial oppression, Sims also painted onto a dark wall an enlarged image of the Woolsack in use in the Canadian Parliament.

On the gallery floor, Blondeau placed a collection of Grandfather Rocks in gathered formation around the Woolsack, a symbol of colonization. On Turtle Island rocks are history keepers and protectors, and guide culturally specific ceremonies. They are also witnessers to ongoing colonization. Blondeau and Sims recognize both the Woolsack and Grandfather Rocks as witnessers, and placed together in close proximity, their different roles and symbolic meanings standing in tension. For the full duration of the exhibition, the rocks provided nourishment to the space as well as protection from the Woolsack. Over time, their presence diminished that sack's potency as a colonial implement.

The installation gave space for Blondeau to activate with performance when she was ready and how she saw fit. In the meantime, the exhibition held art-making workshops, the sharing of food and stories during Métis kitchen table talk events, for fiddle jams and quiet ceremony. Blondeau selected the closing event, named Pishkaapahmisho, which was organized to help send off the artwork in a good way. It began with fiddle music, closing words, and prayers by knowledge keeper Verna DeMontigny. Guests were then guided to the installation space by Métis fiddle player Melissa St. Goddard.

As guests gathered and Goddard quietly played the Red River Jig—an iconic song for lii Michif of this region—an audio track with sounds of nature slowly submerged the fiddle music. While this was happening, Blondeau walked into the *Witnesser* space barefoot, wearing a royal blue dress with a long train. Artist, writer, and curator Jaimie Isaac (Sagkeeng First Nation) walked behind her holding the train of the blue dress, matching her footsteps so both women gently moved in unison with one another. When Blondeau stopped walking for a moment, Isaac would pick up a Grandfather Rock and place it on the dress train with care. These pauses were Isaac's cue to pick up another rock and add to the growing collection. After circling the installation together once, Isaac stepped aside, and Blondeau continued her methodical movement in the space, while struggling with the growing weight of the rocks. At the spot where Isaac first placed a rock on her dress train, Blondeau untied it from the rest of her dress, transforming it into a temporary resting place for the rocks. As she added the rest of the rocks to the pile, sounds of running water consumed the space, and the blue fabric that held the rocks symbolically transformed into a water's edge, where piles of rocks rest partially submerged, as protectors, visitors, and witnessers. As she placed the last of them, the audio track became menacing, as sounds of a moving train emerged and conflicted with the rhythmic and pulsating ones of nature. Once the task was finished, Blondeau emerged from the space, leaving behind the pile of Grandfather Rocks placed beside the Woolsack.

Side by side laid the two types of witnessers—one that would return to a governmental vault to collect dust, and the other to the land, carrying new knowledge from their presence in the show, ready to continue their important role as history keepers, protectors, and ceremony guides.

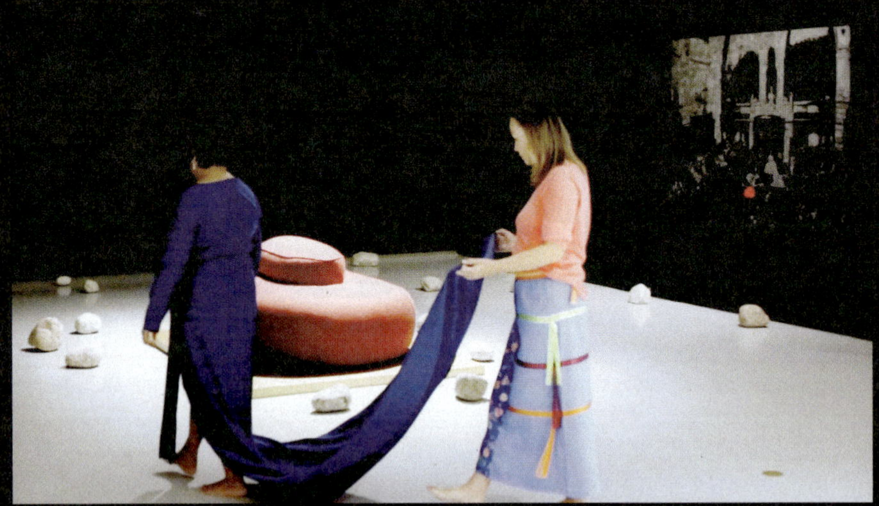

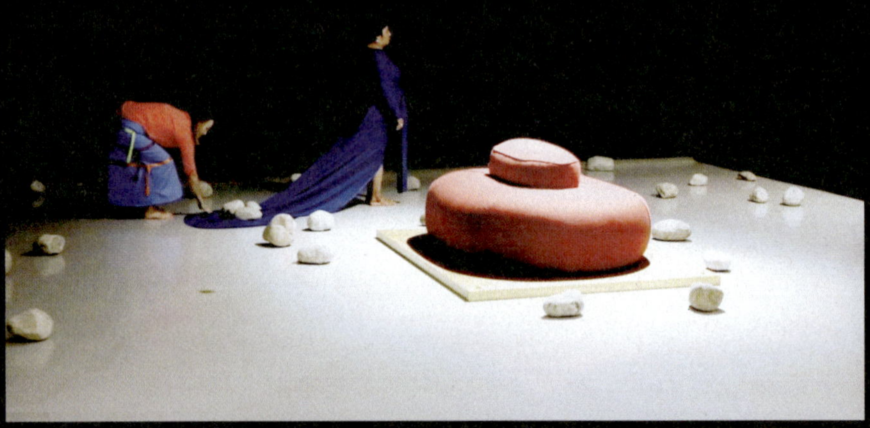

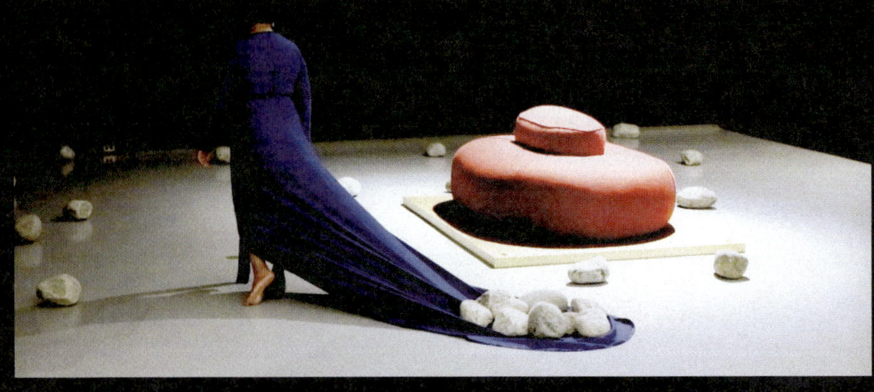

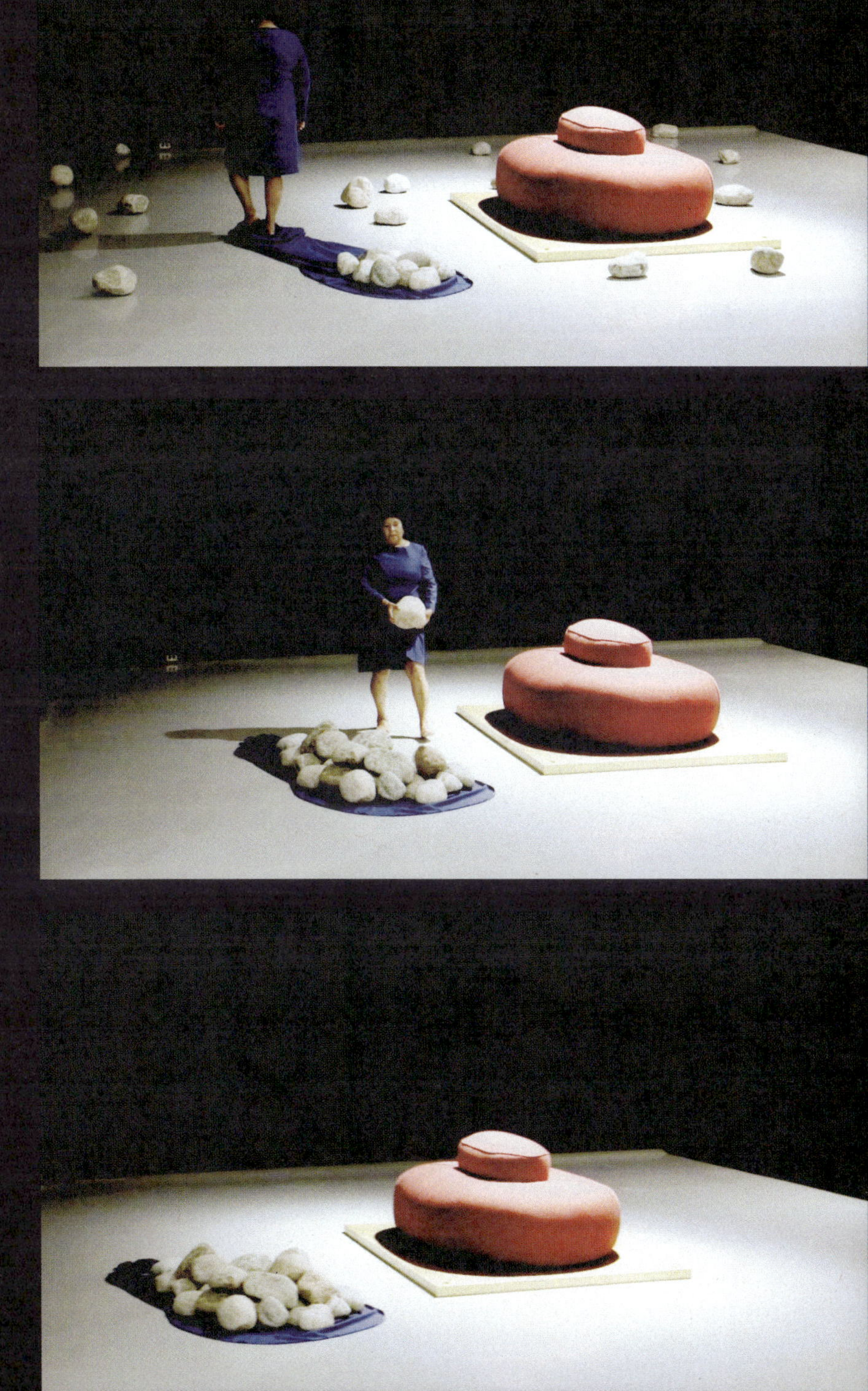

JACKSON 2BEARS

IRON TOMAHAWKS

Jackson 2bears's artistic practice interweaves multimedia performances with interactive installations that address themes of identity, the body, and technology. Begun in 2005, *Iron Tomahawks* is an ongoing, live video performance that utilizes specialized technology to manipulate, edit, and "scratch" audio and video in real time. The performance deconstructs Native stereotypes in popular culture by splicing together disparate forms of media, including clips from Hollywood films, documentaries, Internet videos, and broadcast news. In doing so, he creates new narratives that function as cultural critique, advancing Native modernity through subversion and survivance.

pp. 81–83
Jackson 2bears, *Iron Tomahawks*, 2005–present. Live cinema/scratch video performance artwork, video stills. Photos courtesy of the artist.

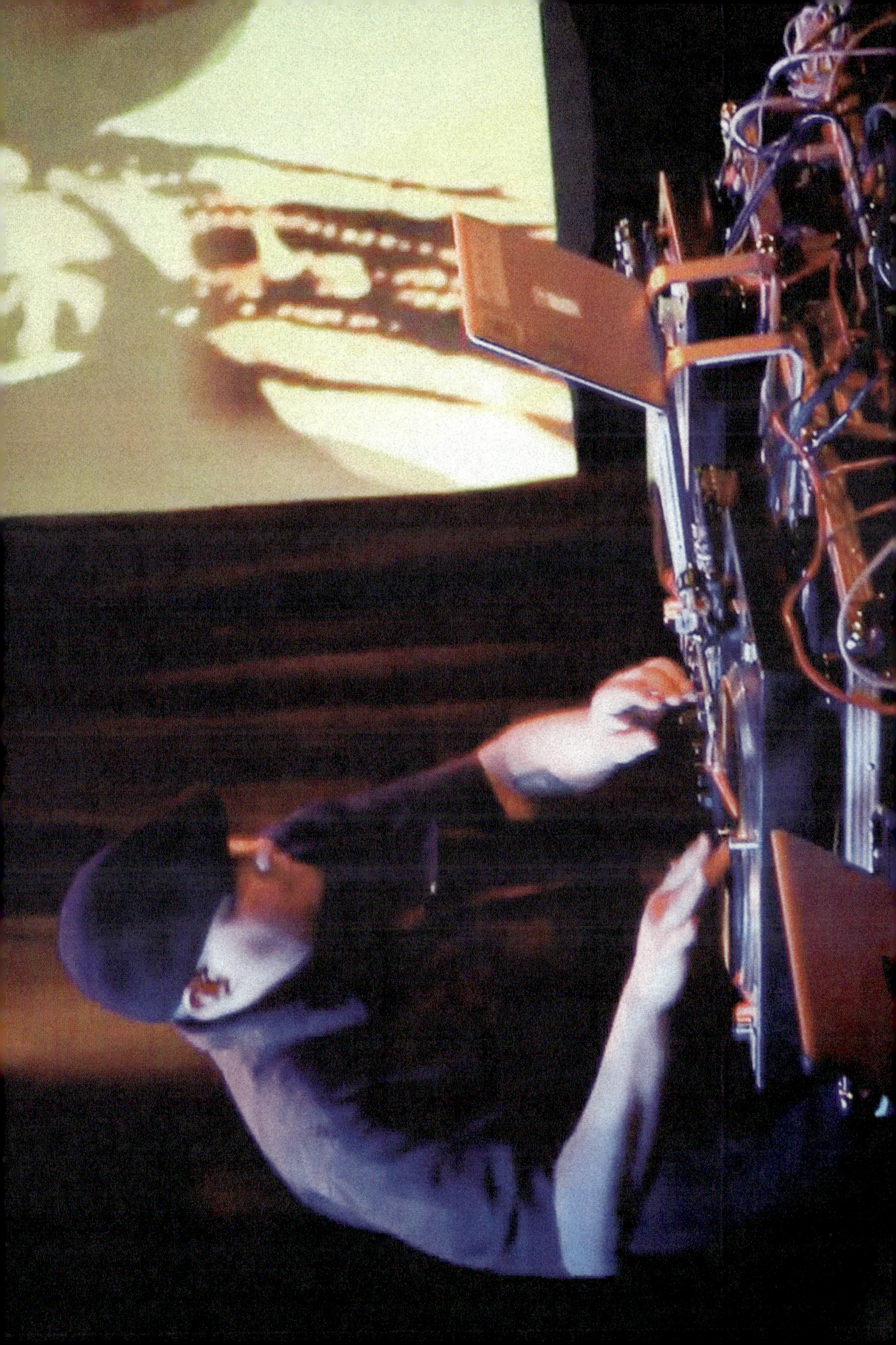

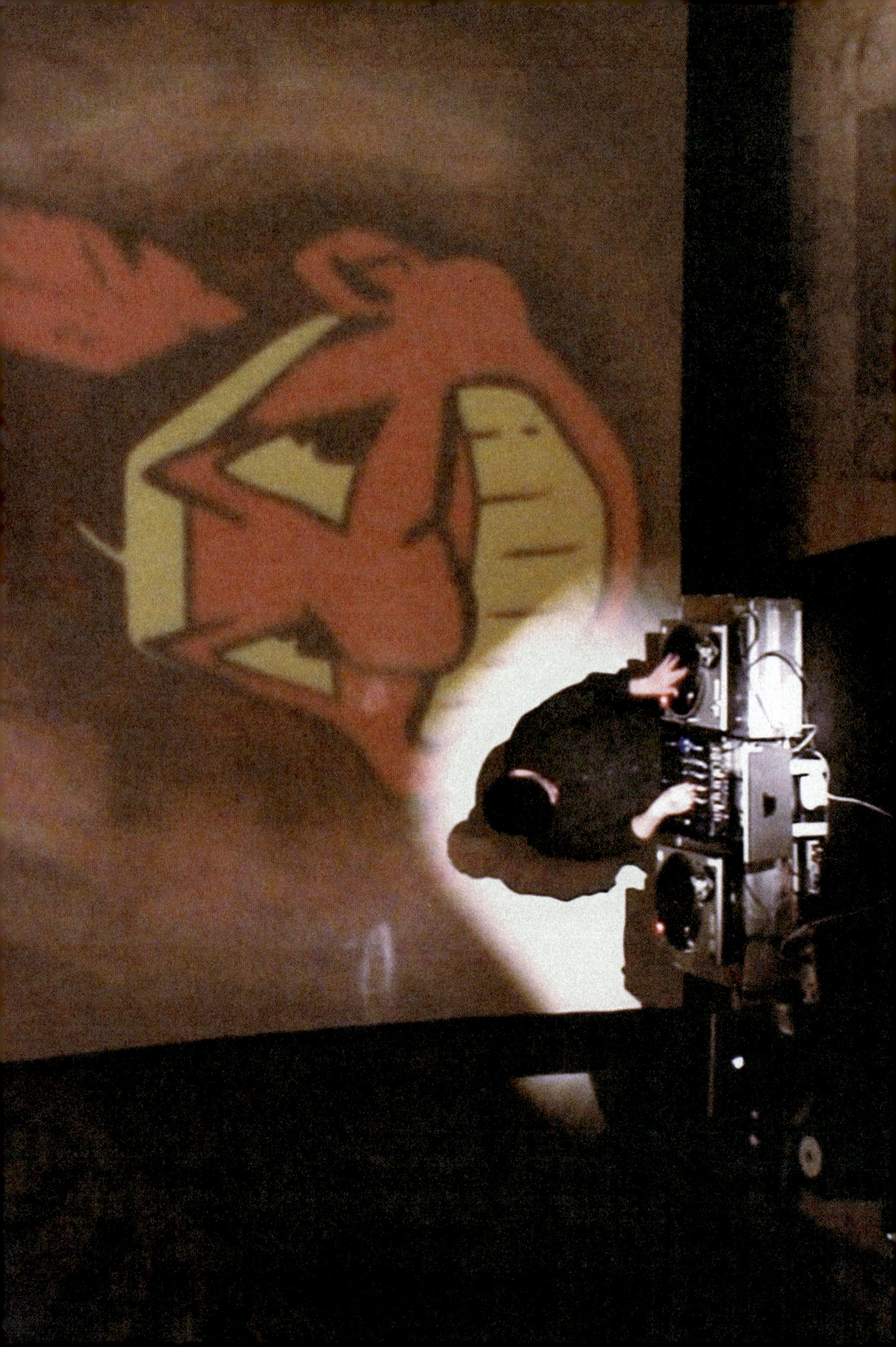

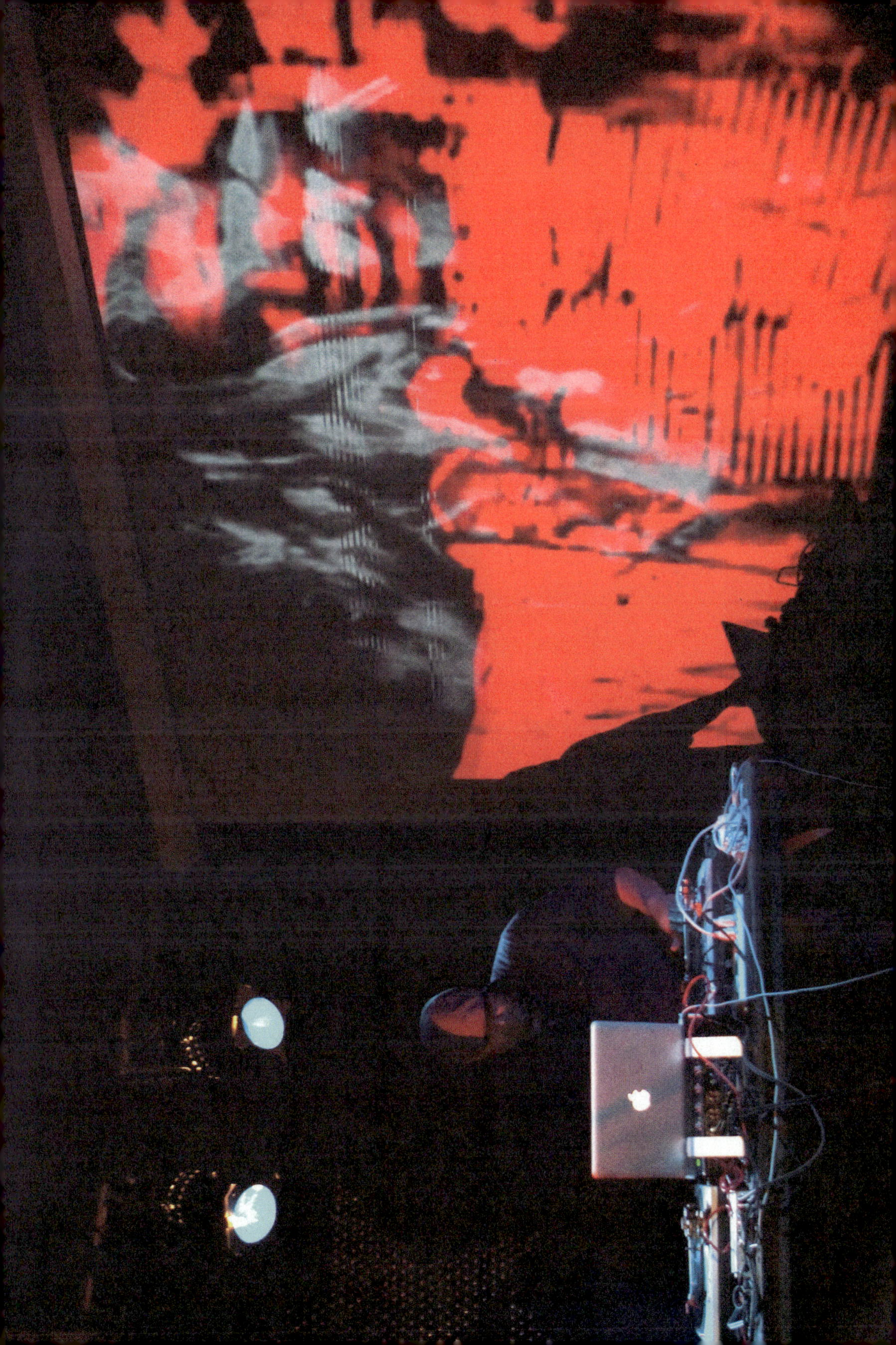

ARCHER PECHAWIS

A BEAR NAMED JESUS

My mother got lost in the woods and never came back.

She went to Auntie Gladys' funeral, and at the service a pack of rabid bears broke in and took my mom. Rabid bears! Right here on the rez! One of the bears was named Jesus, but I'm not sure he was directly involved. It was more like the other bears invoked his name, which obliged him to show up. At any rate, the rabid bears swore they were followers of the bear named Jesus, even as they were dragging him away. He seemed embarrassed by it all.

The rabid bears took my mom and the bear named Jesus to their cave deep in the woods, and forced the bear named Jesus to convince my mom that he was the only light, the only way, the only. I don't know how bears can compel the Son of God, but that's what happened. And even when his heart isn't in it, the bear named Jesus is pretty convincing, so I don't blame my mom for falling for it. Kinda.

But I kinda do. Anyway, these rabid bears were exactly the sort who give nice bears a bad name, and the next thing I knew, this person who looked and sounded like my mom stumbled out of the wilderness, saying all sorts of nonsensical things, at least not coming from my mom. This person claimed (vehemently!) that following the bear named Jesus was the only way to Heaven. I countered that this might be difficult, as the bear named Jesus had been tranquilized by a Conservation Officer and relocated to the bush about a hundred miles north of Stanley Mission. That's a long walk back to the Mistawasis reserve.

Undeterred, this person who looked and sounded like my mom insisted that our ceremonies were the work of the Devil, and anyone participating in them was damned for eternity, and that the bear named Jesus would reappear shortly. She said he was our only hope. I said I hoped he'd stay off the highways.

Imagine my surprise when I heard a tap at the window in the middle of the night. There was the poor old bear named Jesus, all skinny and bedraggled with mats in his fur. He had a bad puncture wound in his side, but it seemed rude to ask where he got it. I let him in and fed him maskihkiy wapoy and pahkwesikan,[1] brushed out his fur, and washed his wounded, bloody paws. He was tired and sad, and kept apologizing for the rabid bears, who he said had good intentions. It may have been unkind, but I reminded him how the road to Hell was built. Then I made him a bunk in the shed. It's not good to let bears sleep in the house.

1 Tea and bannock.

As for my mom I haven't seen her since that fateful day in 1997. The rabid bears continue to abduct people, while the bear named Jesus is collecting CERB[2] and still sleeping in the shed. I tried to get him a job with the rez, but he's not a band member. I've come to love having him around—at night we drink tea and smoke our pipes and laugh while he teaches me how to pray in Cree. As for the person who looks and sounds like my mom, she still makes half-hearted efforts to convert me, but I just pull out my pipe and puff away 'til she gets frightened and leaves.

2 Canada Emergency Response Benefit.

Funny thing, even if he's sitting at the table drinking tea with me, she doesn't seem to recognize the bear named Jesus at all.

MY BROTHER WAS A PROUD MAN

My brother was a proud man.

My brother was a wounded man.

My brother tried to be a good man.

My brother was a sad man.

Who is to blame when the bad medicine takes over, when the medication we self-prescribe becomes worse than the pain that makes us take it? Who is to blame when our families become less important than a dosage? Who is to blame when there is nothing left but blame? Who is to blame when there is nothing left?

Who is to blame?

My brother was a proud man. He was a hard worker, hard enough to overcome the overt racism in the company he worked for to claw his way off the shop floor to middle management. Proud enough to overcome being told he would always have a job on the floor, but there would never be an Indian in management.

Proud enough.

My brother was a wounded man. The slings and arrows of our childhood were always internalized with him, carefully staunching blood with quiet tears. As a child I showed him how drugs could hide the bloodstains, and he took the lesson to heart. I have often felt guilt about this lesson, but the wild teachers were everywhere in our youth, he would have learned one way or another. Best it was me he chased around the house with a butcher knife on his first trip. Family should stay close.

Wounded enough?

My brother was a good man. His heart was a refuge of good intentions, and these would leak out, a disarming quiet kindness springing from the trees. He loved his children fiercely until the last day of his life, when the drugs had won him over so completely he forgot his own son's birthday.

Good enough?

My brother was a sad man. His sadness emanated from him, a pall that no amount of wicked Cree humor could sweep away. But his game face was strong: most would not have felt the Chernobyl at his core. After I cleaned up I tried and tried to get inside him, to drag him to a 12 Step meeting, therapy, anything, but the half-life of crack was too strong.

My brother tried to be a good man. He did not deserve a drug addict's death, murdered by the dealers he worked for. At the end he was lost to us, to the world, to himself.

My brother tried to be a good man.

KITE

TAKE CARE MY BOY

Score for hair-braid AI interface, bottle of mezcal, six months of field recordings, and the last conversations you will have with your grandfathers.

pp. 96–97
Kite, *Take Care My Boy*, 2021. Performance with AI hair-braid interface, video and audio samples, violin, and Minitaur Analog Bass Synthesizer, 19:28 minutes, video stills. Photos courtesy of the artist.

A violin sits alone on the floor of a theater
Sing Yiddish vocables "dy dy dy"
A violin plays an open D
A violinist begins to play the tune from my paternal aunt, Alicia Svigals', album
A disembodied hand braids hair
A slow synth is beating an ultra low tone
Open a bottle of Mezcal

The violin grinds to a roar
Returns to a ghostly open D
Before being interrupted by Alicia's voice
"The past and the distant past, all of the possibilities for you and the future were infinite,
and as time went on and things happened, it narrowed and narrowed until the actual you was created.
This specific you, out of all the yous that could have been.
So as you go on, your possibilities in the future expand and expand. In the future there are infinite possibilities.
So, possibilities for your fate, future, and life, as time goes on, widen and widen until they are infinite. Isn't that nice?"
My paternal grandfather Edwin replies, "Nice."
Alicia continues, "I experienced this…"

Your body sways to the beat
Have a drink of Mezcal
A thumb piano-like sound echos and repeats
Braid controls Feedback/Dry/Wet
As your body presses back and forth, the hair braid sways, deepening the sonic changes
A young man says "Chair solo of a lifetime."
Smoke a cigarette
Three women sing off-key,
"Let me be the one for you
And I want to spend my life with you."
They laugh.
Braid controls Reverb/Dry/Wet
"Let me be the one for you

And I want to spend my life with you."
They laugh.

Braid controls Chorus Amount/Rate/Dry/Wet
"Let me be the one for you
And I want to spend my life with you."
They laugh.
Braid controls Erosion Freq/Amt
"Let me be the one for you
And I want to spend my life with you."
They laugh.
Braid controls Downsample

A too-slow breakbeat starts to layer
Jungle samples incessant in the right ear
Have another shot of Mezcal
Braid controls Frequency sweep of Town Bass sample
A woman's hands turn synthesizer knobs
Dance like the liquor just kicked in at a DnB show
Dance up to the camera person, dance around them

A slow zoom to a spider
Do I worship at the spider altar?
The hair braid controls samples playing, triggering their repetitions

A computerized voice says,
"So for writers perform as a kind of subtext, suggesting their engagement with the characters' thoughts. Here's not about watching, but listening to, and for time, unknowable time sources. It is possible to give a precise description of [distortion] 6,625 and the net effect it has on our government's access to raw data from the military. For our purposes, it is important to remember that the for time, unknowable time, ceases. Wait and watch. You will know when time is no longer time. Wait and watch.
No time.

Have you ever just wanted something so badly you would cut your own chest open and dig your own grave in the dusty earth, on the hill in South Dakota? Laid down to be filled with maggots and embraced by the earth for time unknowable? This is what this is about. Revenge. The use of a toxin to cause pain and death to someone you love. You got what you wanted, John. I'm very sorry I was too late to save you. But I won't beg you.

Have you ever just wanted something so badly you would cut your own chest open and dig your own grave in the dusty earth, on the hill in South Dakota? Laid down to be filled with maggots and embraced by the earth for time unknowable? That's what I want. That's what I have for you. I want to experience every moment and look back over my shoulder in the morning from somewhere where I no longer feel like a failure.

[Distortion in the narration] I want to eat—cut your own chest open and dig your own grave dusty earth on a hill in South Dakota. Lay down filled with maggots and embraced by the earth for time unknowable? Be assured that the heavens do not know and so there is no purpose or sense to your actions. Your life is only a small sliver in eternity and there is nothing that you can do at this moment. T for tiiiiiiiime unknowable.
Time ceases.
Embraced by the earth on the hill. Dig your own grave, mother, or make us dig our own graves for survival.
Listen to the earth, the only one who breathes. The only one who can hear. The pulse of life. The heart of the Universe, held high. For time unknowable—cut your chest open. Breathe in the dirt. You can crawl away. Get out and go home."

Mahpiya Nazin says, "I got what I got, and there ain't nothing I can do about it."

"They really have a hard time understanding, these medicine men, that there are certain things you have to do to get to where you're at. You can't go play games with people."

Say, "I went around, talked to lots of people about stones this week. Really interesting stuff, the experiences people had about kept stones and electricity."

And endless reverb in the left ear.
Have a sip of Mezcal.

A man sniffles

Mahpiya Nazin says, "Well, that's what happens to medicine men... He's a good kid, he tried to help a lot of people, but he just doesn't understand the simplicity of life, how simple it really is."

The bass synth overtakes the voice
Braid controls Overdrive Dry/Wet

"He tried yuwipi but they wouldn't untie him, so he stayed tied up. And I asked 'well, did you have a dream or anything?' He said 'Yeah' or something. You hear the elk talking? Told him what he had to do. I don't know if he got it, but he supposedly tied up last night at the yuwipi. Couldn't get untied. It felt like it just fell off. The blanket and the ties.

The braid controls the LFO amount.

"They feel like when they tied up like that…" [low frequencies take over the soundscape].

"They told me how beautiful life can be for everyone. The whole, the whole United States. The whole country. Around the world, if people would just wake up, they're all asleep. Every humankind walks this earth for a reason."

Mahpiya Nazin says, "You guys have a long drive."

“Do some amazing things the spirits tell me.”

He says to the young white man,
“I look at people cause I see things.”
“Things will take you where it’s supposed to.”
“You take care my son.”

Braid controls Chance of Glitch
Braid controls breakcore sample “GOLDEN BOY” Buffer
Shuffler 2.0 Dry/Wet

An elder arm wrestles a young white man

A crying family cuts off all your hair
Have one last drink

(high pitched chorus)
Rock bottom here we come La la la la la
Rock bottom here i go La la la la la
(slowed)
Rock bottom here we come La la la la la
Rock bottom here i go La la la la la
(slowed further)
Rock bottom here we come La la la la la
Rock bottom here i go La la la la la
(and slowed further)
Rock bottom here we come La la la la la
Rock bottom here i go La la la la la
(and slowed further)
Rock bottom here we come La la la la la
Rock bottom here i go La la la la la
(and slowed further)
Rock bottom here we come La la la la la
Rock bottom here i go La la la la la

For my grandfathers

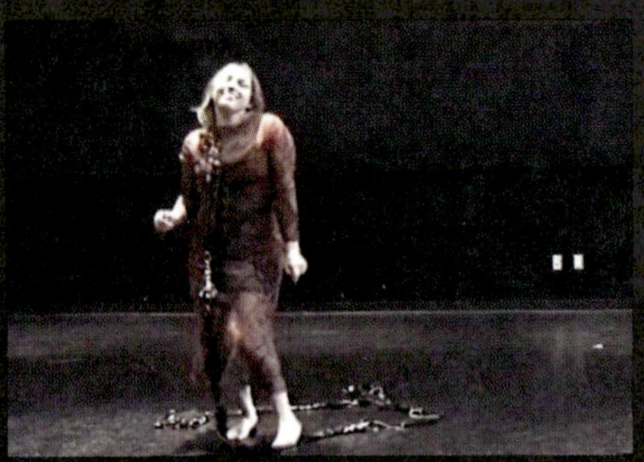

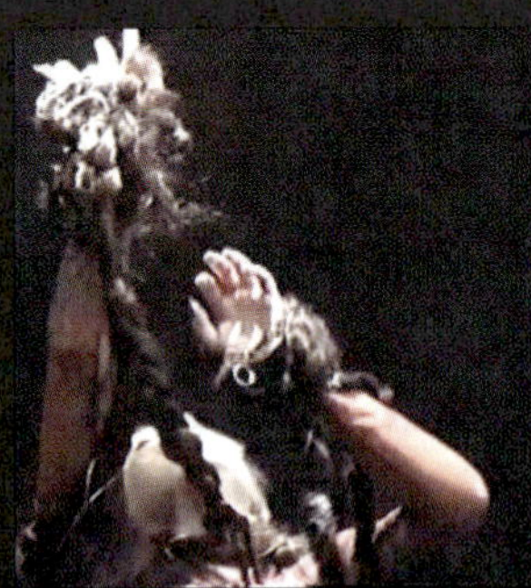

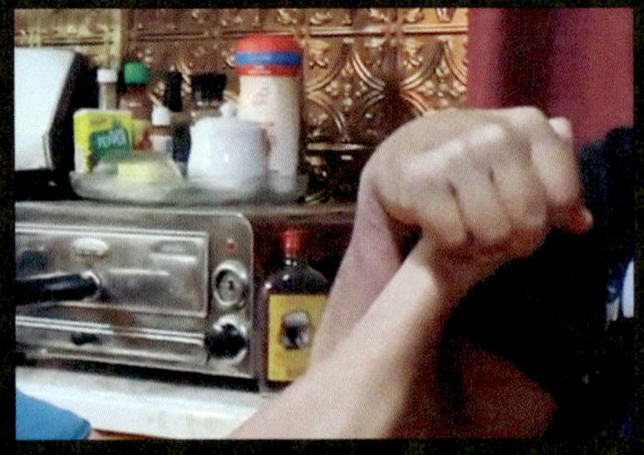

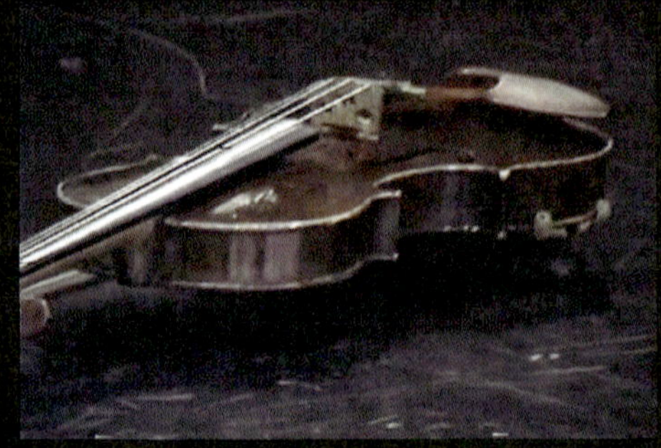

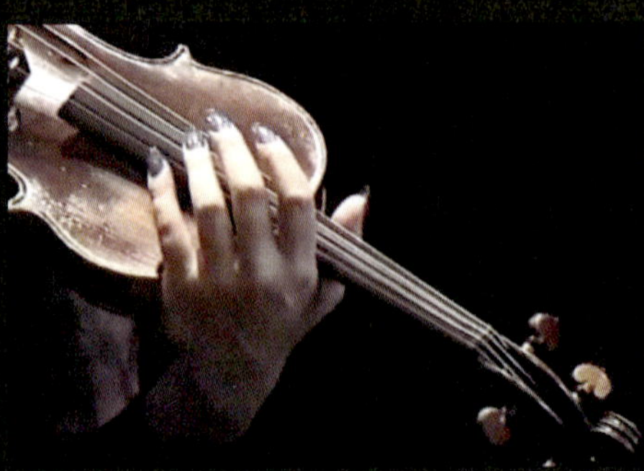

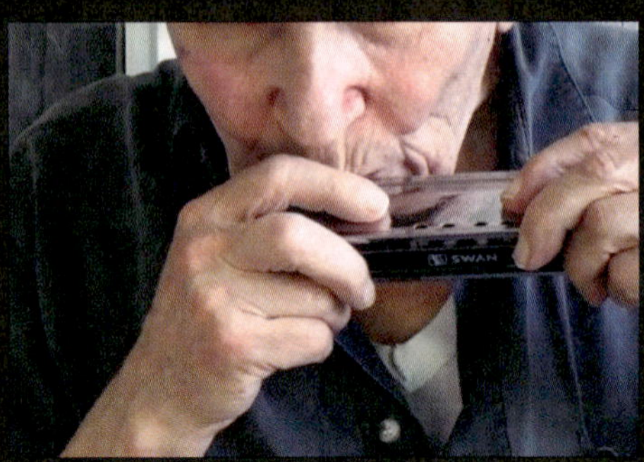
SWAN

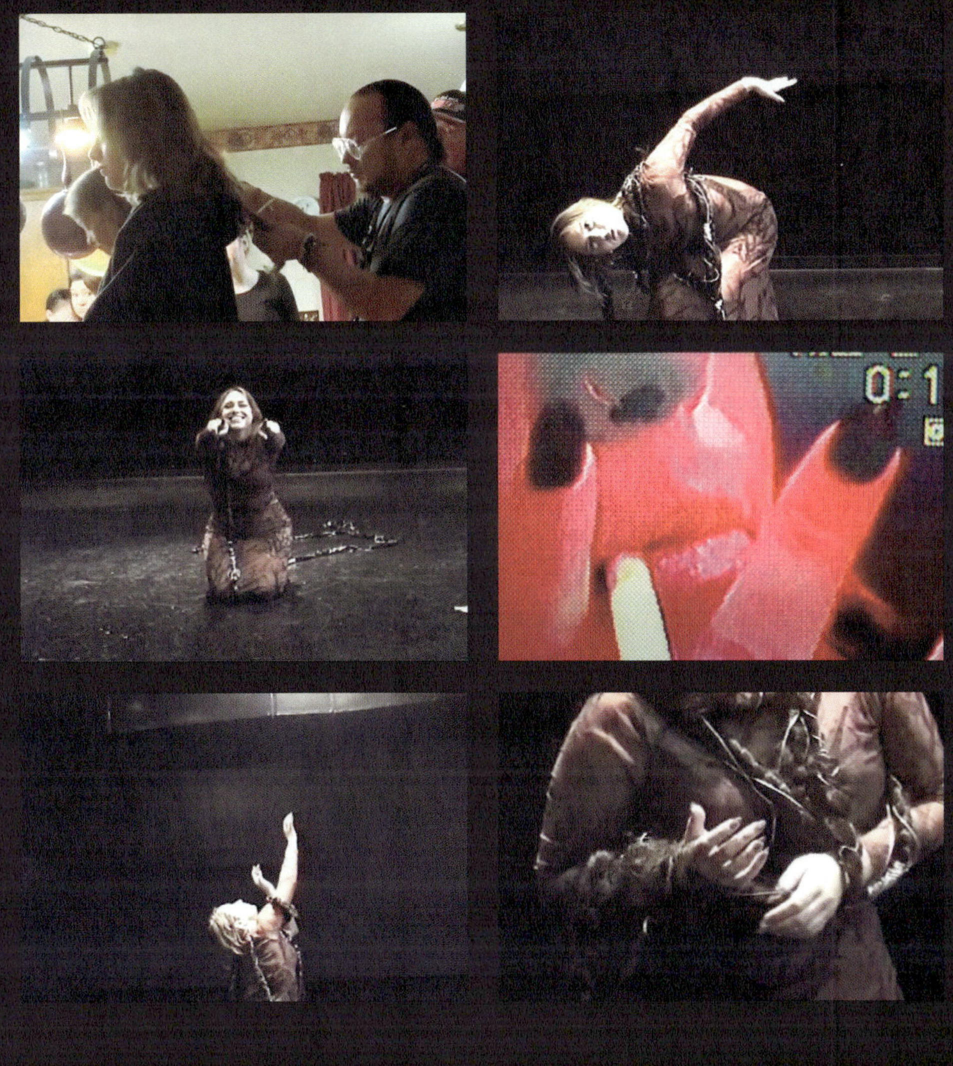

CHARLENE VICKERS

MY DRAWINGS ARE SHAKING UNDER THE MANHATTAN BRIDGE

Through painting, sculpture, and performance, multidisciplinary urban Anishinaabe Kwe artist Charlene Vickers focuses on color, healing, land, Indigenous presence, and embodied connections to her birthplace. In her 2022 performance *My Drawings Are Shaking Under the Manhattan Bridge*, Vickers creates a live, reverberating synth soundscape within an installation of line drawings from her series *Ancestor Gesture: Diviners*. As the pulsating sounds scratch, layer, and build, Vickers envelops herself in the music by gently raking the portable soundboard over her arms, head, and chest. In concert with the music, the drawings form an accumulation of "careful repetitions of moments, movements, of motions and emotions," as the artist notes in the accompanying score, conjuring her own experiences, somatic responses, as well as metaphysical landscapes, and encapsulating them in an acoustic environment. Through her performance, Vickers evokes the abstract process of memory work—with acts of repetition, automatic movement, and bodily immersion, she illustrates a way of encountering the past through an embodied experience, reflecting the way histories are felt, remembered, and carried across spatial and temporal distances to connect ancestral knowledge with the present.

pp. 99–101
Charlene Vickers, *My Drawings Are Shaking Under the Manhattan Bridge*, 2022. Performance presented at New Art Dealers Alliance (NADA) project space, April 24, 2022, video stills and ink on paper drawing. Photos courtesy of the artist.

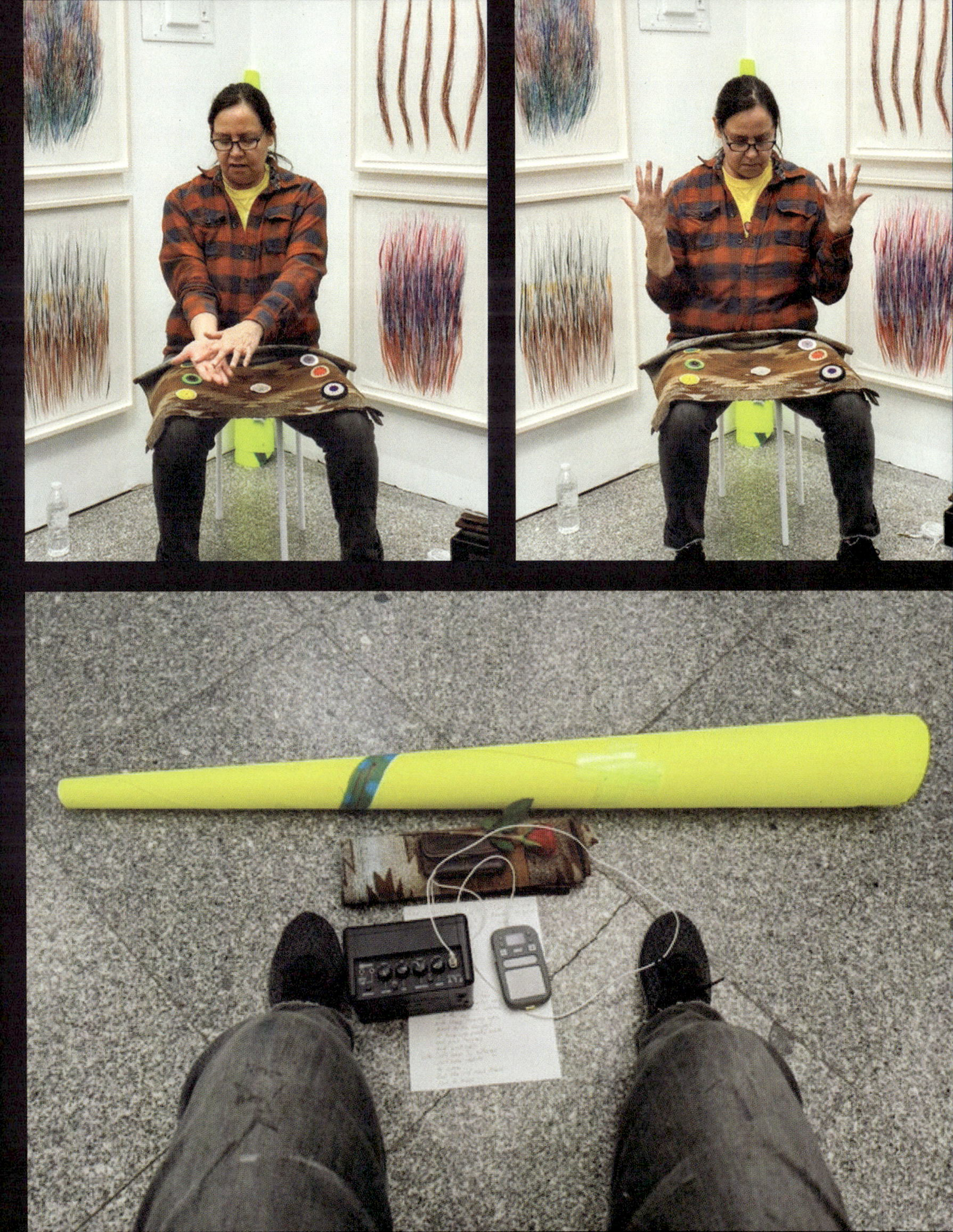

My drawings are shaking
under the Manhattan Bridge

My breathe is there
in the fine lines
The careful repetitions
of moments
movements
of motions + emotions

At the points between
the lines
and my hands (3x)

1. Breath Memory
Being
Her Being
Breath
(3x)

- Objects
- Blanket

2. Take out
Wallet w beads
Lay on body

3. Lay out +
turn over.

I am sitting in a memory. At the back of a field. On my Gramma's farm. We sit in the long grass. Talking and pulling stalks out of the earth. Pulling + picking the seeds. Chewing the green. A sweet green marrow. The bees buzz through the makeshift nest, sitting cross legged, like the old people did. The ones before us. The original people with wide brown hands. Strong everything.

(side profile, hand pray) hit arms

✓WOLF SIRENS 92
SOFT LEAD 19
DIST. GUITAR 33
~~POWER CHORD 82~~
2) SYNTH BASS 48
WOBBLE BASS 48
DIST. BASS 39

✓✓ RESONATE 95
✓ HELICOPTER 96
1) DIDGERIDOO 32

- Get the cone
Ready to point
- hear
- look
- listen to the
GROUND.
- Breathe into
the drawings.
- Put it down
- START
THE SYNTH

There were fine lines
Framing her fearful eyes
The original ones watched
Out for her
With sharp knowing eyes
Alert to the dangers
Of those with pointed white
and pink tongues
And pink eyes
With Soft ears so alluring
Just some rabbits
to some
But the old ones knew
Not to trust.

URSULA JOHNSON

A FEW WORDS

Be professional
Be kind
This is your job
You will make a work that will put you on the map
Documentation is everything
Make sure to take good documentation
If you're not a photographer hire a photographer that is their job and their art practice and you do your art practice by supporting them as they will support you everyone specializes in something and we'll need to work together to create a healthy strong network
Create relationships with different Artists, Administrators, Technicians, Preparators, Conservators, Registrars, Curators, Directors, Managers, Collectors, etc.
Create a working CV
Create a selected works CV
Create a one page CV
Create a Bio
Create a short Bio
Create a shorter Bio
Don't forget to update
Show up to other Artists openings
Show up for other Artists
While you are in school you are often too busy to go to different openings, talks, lectures, workshops but once you leave school this will be your life
Go to openings
Go to talks
Go to lectures
Go to workshops
Show up for other artists
This is your life
This is your family
Be professional
Be kind
This is your job
Treat others the way you want to be treated
When you go to new places show up as if you are going to a job interview

Because that is your job interview
Develop ethics
Develop values
Practice your ethics
Practice your values
Do not take things personally
It's not personal
Do not be afraid to talk about money
Talk about money
Join artist organizations, like CARFAC (Canadian Artists' Representation/Le Front des artistes canadiens)
They are your advocates
Review contracts
Amend contracts
Review the amendments
Sign the contract
Do not talk about works in progress–unless you are looking for advice
You will get advice
We all give advice
Do not talk about processes or materials you are working with–unless you are looking for advice
You will get advice
We all give advice
Do talk about the subject matter
The subject matter is important
Art is important
Art can make a difference
Art makes a difference
Art can feel lonesome
You will work alone
We all work alone
You will work with others
We all work with others
You will work with a team
We all work with teams
Technicians and preparators are your best friends
Take care of them like your best friends
They will be your best friends
They are your best friends

Be professional
Be kind
This is your job

Written in 2020 by Ursula Johnson at
the Koerner Residency

PELENAKEKE BROWN

SCORES FROM ONE RECOVERING TOKENIZED BROWN PERSON TO ANOTHER

A SCORE FROM ONE RECOVERING TOKENIZED BROWN PERSON TO ANOTHER

Your integrity as a person should never be compromised for the institution.⋆

How to loosen that lump in your throat and survive that meeting.⋆

Remember, you are your ancestors' wildest dreams.

When something occurs where the lump appears and starts to grow:

1. As it rises, speak up and voice your discomfort as it happens (it will get smaller that way).
2. If in doubt of what to say, repeat what they said and ask, "What did you mean by what you said?"
3. If it is not safe to speak up within the institution, practice saying no outside of the workplace.
4. Experiment with saying no.
5. Keep practicing, upping the ante until you can take this skill into the boardroom.⋆
6. There is language and skill to these interactions—ask other Indigenous and Black/Brown people in leadership for advice on how to frame and speak their language.
7. Remember, every time you speak-up-in-action, the lump cannot grow. It is like fire—do not allow it space (or oxygen) to grow.

Practice saying these phrases:

"I'm not sure that I am available, let me get back to you."
"No, that doesn't suit me."
"What you just said made me feel uncomfortable. What did you mean by it?"
"Why did you assume that I am not the manager?"

"You can direct your questions to me, I am the Director."
"Are you noticing that you keep cutting me off?"
"Why did you say that?"

⋆ replace this word with whatever white-dominated space you are in.

A SCORE TO SURVIVE TOKENIZATION

Find a body of water.
>>   >>   >>   >>   >>

If you can submerge yourself, please do so.

:: :: :: :: :: :: :: :: :: :: :: :: :: ::

Let her wash over you.

<<   <<   <<   <<   <<

Float.

::< >::

If you can't submerge yourself:

Take in your surroundings.

\ | /

Notice the water in front of you.

>>   >>   >>   >>   >>

Does the water move?

//> //>//> //> //> //> //

Is there a current you can witness?

//> //> //> //> //> //< \\ <\\ <\\ <\\< \\< \\< \\

How does the light hit the water?

;;

Listen to the sound of the shore

[][][][][][][][][][][][][][]

Finally, breathe in:

= = = = =

Taste, smell her.

<><><><><><>

Rinse and repeat.

Some advice while recovering from burnout caused by tokenization.
Remember:

Before the light appears there is always darkness.
You are magic, powerful, and almighty.
It will get better.

You may feel numb immediately after.
It's ok to watch Netflix all day.
It's ok to cry a lot.
Get a shower seat to make crying in the shower easier.

You may focus on what went wrong and why, try writing out these realizations as they come to you.
Look up the "glass cliff phenomenon."
Your immediate family and loved ones may find it

difficult to keep listening to you speaking about the toxicity. If this occurs, find others you can speak to. You'll be surprised to know that more people than you realize have gone through similar situations.

It's ok to go quiet and retreat.
Focus on small daily tasks such as creating quiet rituals for yourself in the home.
Get a plant.

Read your favorite authors.
Go back to hobbies that you have always loved.
Spend time with your family, especially kids, they always think you are incredible no matter what you do.
When you re-enter the workforce, you may still be recovering. It is ok to go slow.

Remember:
Before the light appears there is always darkness.
You are magic, powerful, and almighty.
It will get better.

And if all else fails, remember:

"We sweat and cry saltwater, so we know that the ocean is really in our blood."
—Teresia Teaiwa

A score to soothe the soul

How are you

marking time + space?

How did your ancestors

mark time + space?

ROSANNA RAYMOND

WE ARE THE VĀ/NOW

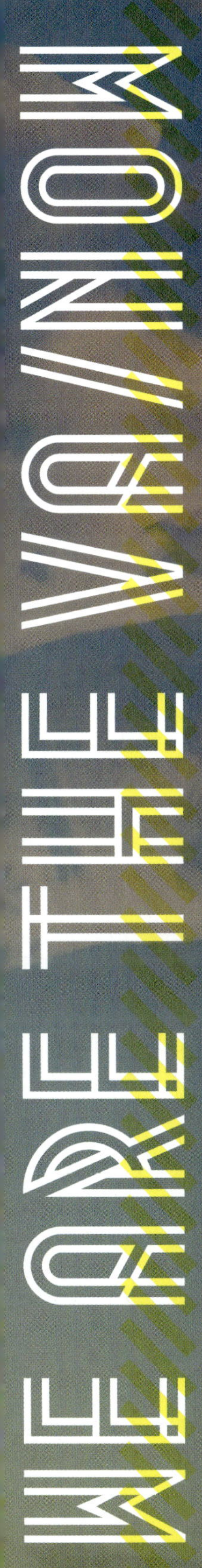

I CRY THE OCEAN
I BLEED THE EARTH
I SLEEP WITH MOUNTAINS
I GREET YOU WITH MY DEAD

MAY MY WATERS GREET YOUR WATERS
MAY MY MOUNTAINS GREET YOUR MOUNTAINS
MAY MY HOUSE GREET YOUR HOUSE
MAY MY PEOPLE GREET YOUR PEOPLE

Greetings to Ngāti Whātua who keep the fires warm, tendering the mana of the whenua, where I take shelter, Tāmaki Makaurau, Te Ika a Maui, Aotearoa. Ma le alofa ma le agaga fa'afetai.

Greetings to the weavers of this publication, bringing us together to share some time and space with each other. Fa'afetai ma le viiga.

Let us take this time to acknowledge those who have passed, for we are the past, we are the present, we are the future... we are the Vā/NOW.

SAVĀGE K'LUB HAKA

COMPOSED AND GIFTED TO THE SAVĀGE K'LUB BY PRECIOUS CLARK, (NGĀTI WHĀTUA, WAIKATO, TE URI O HAU, NGĀTI HE AND PĀKEHĀ), 2015

Ngā Iwi Taketake	INDIGENOUS PEOPLES
Maranga Ake Ra	RISE UP
Ngā Ringatoi Taketake	INDIGENOUS ARTISTS
Maranga Ake Ra	RISE UP
Wānangahia Te Mātauranga	DEEPLY LEARN AND UNDERSTAND KNOWLEDGE
Karawhuia O Pakiwaitara	THROW, DISPERSE YOUR STORIES
Kōrerohia	SHARE TALK
Rarangatia	WEAVE
Ka Tiritiria	PLANT IT
Ka Poupoua	CEMENT AND EMBED IT
Hikitia Te Ihi Me Te Wana	LIFT THE ESSENTIAL FORCE AND AWE
Tū Heru Hāpai	STAND PROUD WITH YOUR HERU COMB HIGH
Māhunga Tikitiki	WITH PROUDLY DISPLAYED TOPKNOT
Haumi E	PLUG THE WAKA WITH THE LAST WOOD CHIP
Hui E	GATHER TOGETHER IN UNITY
Tāiki E!	IT IS DONE!

ACTI.VĀ.TOR

Performative agent, using the vā as a methodology to bring the past into the present, creating a space of connection and cohesion.

CONSER.VĀ.TION

Sustaining and maintaining past, present, and future relationships, not just the physical condition of a thing.

CULTI.VĀ.TOR

Relational Researcher, employing culturally appropriate ways to establish links — genealogical, geographical, historical, and social.

EXCESSIFICATION

To be visually hectic, to celebrate abundance.

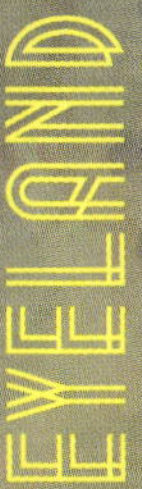

The cultural and political geography of my surroundings as seen through my eyes.

FAB.RICATOR

Creative native, dreaming, gathering, designing, fashioning, constructing, composing, writing, rehearsing, installing stuff and things.

NIU AITU

Fully formed, fleshed-out urban charismas that embody the mauli and the mana of the fāgogo and gafa they relay.

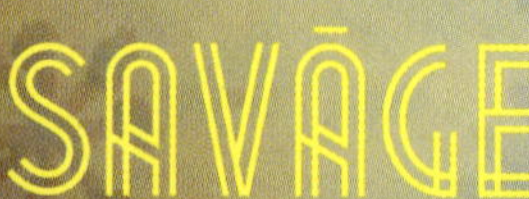

SAVĀGE

Unthinking or rethinking the savage, the capitalisation of VĀ privileges the Samoan notion of vā, which I evoke to maintain the mana of Moana-based practices and protocols at the heart of my creative practice.

VĀ

An active space, that binds people and things together, forming relationships that necessitate reciprocal obligations.

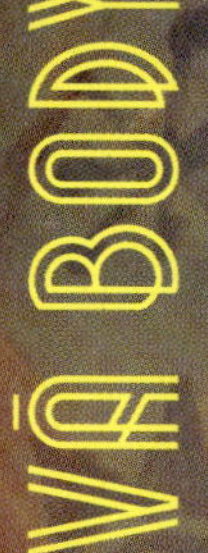

VĀ BODY

A corporeal vessel that shares time and space with the genealogical past, present, and future. A non-gendered body or space where all ancestors are housed, both male and female, atua and aitu.

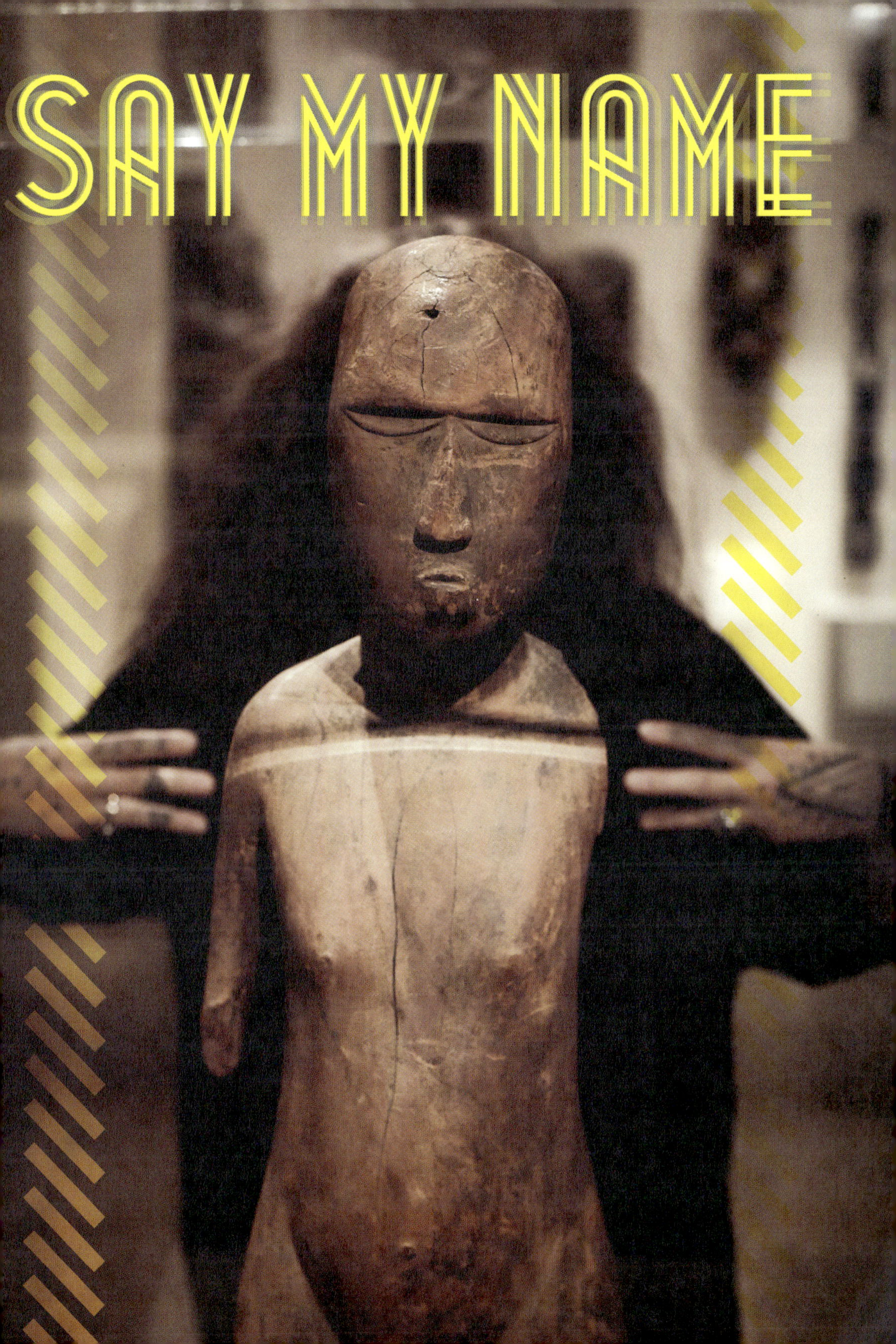
SAY MY NAME

Speaking through the mouths of priests
THE GODS ARE CALLING

They are gasping for air
BREATHING IN GLASS
Running out of breath

They have been **STRIPPED NAKED**, publicly exposed
MUTILATED

Now demanding assimilation

Come gather ... **ENTER**
Through my womb

I will take the tapu ... **TURN IT INTO BLOODLINES**

If I have to I will eat my own flesh
Scrape my own **BONES**

The tension feeds me
Like the voracious **APPETITE OF THE ATUA**

PROSTRATE YOURSELVES while I
Nourish them with the body of a brown Christ

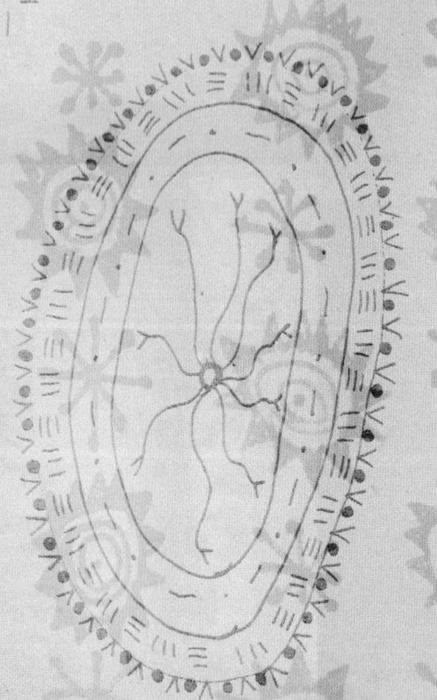

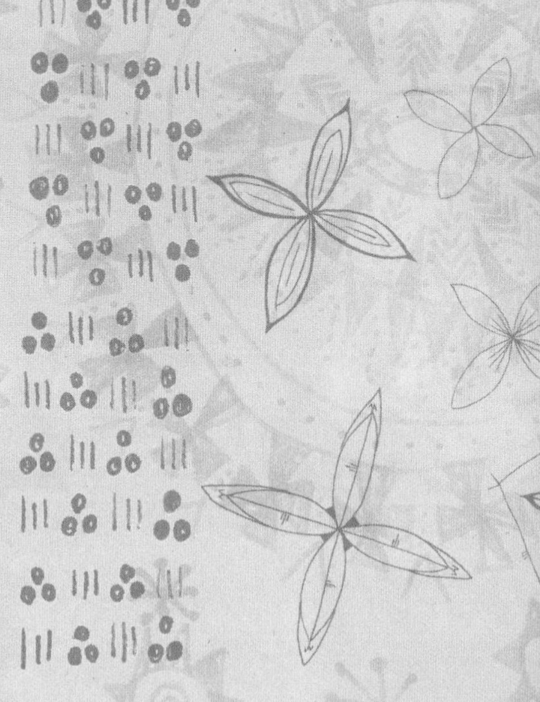

Open your legs ... **PROTECT ME**

I ask for nothing
but to sit in my **OWN WOMB**

My waters have broken
RE—BIRTHING
Forgotten pantheons

They bear **WOMEN'S** names
In **BODIES** that carry no shame

Created in the rays of the **MILKY WAY** ... Hine Rau Renga
In the **WAVES OF THE SEA** ... Hine Moana
By **RED CLAY**...Hine Ahu One

Deified ... Kihawahine ... Hikule'o ... Nafanua
Celestial ... Mareikura ... Tapuitea

WhakaRONGO mai

WE ARE ONE AND THE SAME

So say my name

I'll stop the **WINDS**
And you will never have to **PRAY** in his name again

CHARLES KORONEHO

TE TOKI HARURU (THE RESOUNDING ADZE)

pp. 124–25
Charles Koroneho/Te Toki Haruru, *Ko Te Ākau*, 2021. Multimedia installation, presented in collaboration with Filament Eleven 11; Nelson Arts Festival at Ars Electronica Garden: Aotearoa; Creative New Zealand; Linz, Austria, April 2022. Photos courtesy of the artist.

I was made into a pou and given a function to perform. My form was shaped according to that function and I became an object of culture, my eyes rolled back into their sockets, tongue protruding, hands and body trembling. After every breath, I expelled a noise and willingly accepted instruction. Many marks adorned my form, and I was captured.

I was positioned in a place between my function and the world, it transformed me into a rock, then a bird and I settled on branches that were different. I become unraveled and anxious, prey to difference. I will consume myself and offer up an escape for change. I chose performance to understand restriction, negotiate its contentious site, and step into accepting my anxiety.

The adze can also shape and form a pou, that I desire.

--

Te Toki Haruru is a conceptual platform created to explore Indigenous ceremonial practices, intercultural collaboration, and the intersection between dance, theater, visual arts, and design. These concepts are at the heart of *Te Toki Haruru* and are the means by which I examine the collision between Māori cosmology, New Zealand society, and global cultures.

The cosmological origins of bodies, both celestial and terrestrial, from the ancestral stories of Aotearoa mediate my understanding of how Indigenous creativity and performance inform my creative practice. Receiving formal training in contemporary dance, choreography, and performance consolidated a research pathway toward the ancestral body, creating the contestable landscape of resistance and inquiry by which I currently explore the precipice of Indigenous performance making.

My creative practice is founded on the desire to understand how ceremony functions in the creation of cultural space and why Indigenous bodies occupy and inhabit this space. In the cultural context of my community, this is best observed in funeral practices where grief, bereavement, and lamentation reveal bodies in ceremonial and spiritual stasis. The concept of temporary death spaces as experienced in funerals, is an example of how a body can have spiritual agency and cosmological significance.

The research I am exploring is *Tua o Te Ārai*—beyond the veil, after death. The primary direction I am developing re-addresses the space of mourning.

I am working with four conceptual spaces:
Urupā—burial ground, cemetery, graveyard (customary
Atamira—an elevated platform for the dead, corpse (remembered)
Tūāhu—ceremonial platform, sacred place (nearly forgotten)
Te Ārai—a threshold, resting place for the dead (unknown)

From these conceptual spaces I created *Ko Te Ākau*—poetics of land, water and sky.

Ākau is where the ocean meets the land, the horizon connects land, water, and sky. A meeting place of difference, the in-between and situational, an encounter with duration and the ephemeral, an unlikely collaboration to the formation of new spaces, the performance of community, poetry, and ancestral bodies.

Ko Te Ākau is a visual arts installation and curated performance program for live and virtual spaces, created for group and solo performances, within a design accurate installation of lighting, sound design, and video projection.

The kaupapa of the work is best served by “Mātiro Whakamua,” looking beyond the horizon. The project is aesthetically futuristic and abstract, a vehicle for past, present, and future manifestations, performed by the living ancestral body of the artist. In this shared space, performances transport us through remembrance, acknowledgement, and aspiration. The hope of a poetic land, water, and sky is the horizon carried by the kaupapa, where the optimism and guidance of a human being in ceremonial performance places our imagination amongst the cosmos.

Te Toki Haruru projects resemble an anthology—as a collation of cultural detritus at the aftermath of colonization and a survey of cultural loss, its impact on our present lives is measured through the shifting parameters of creativity, art, and politics.

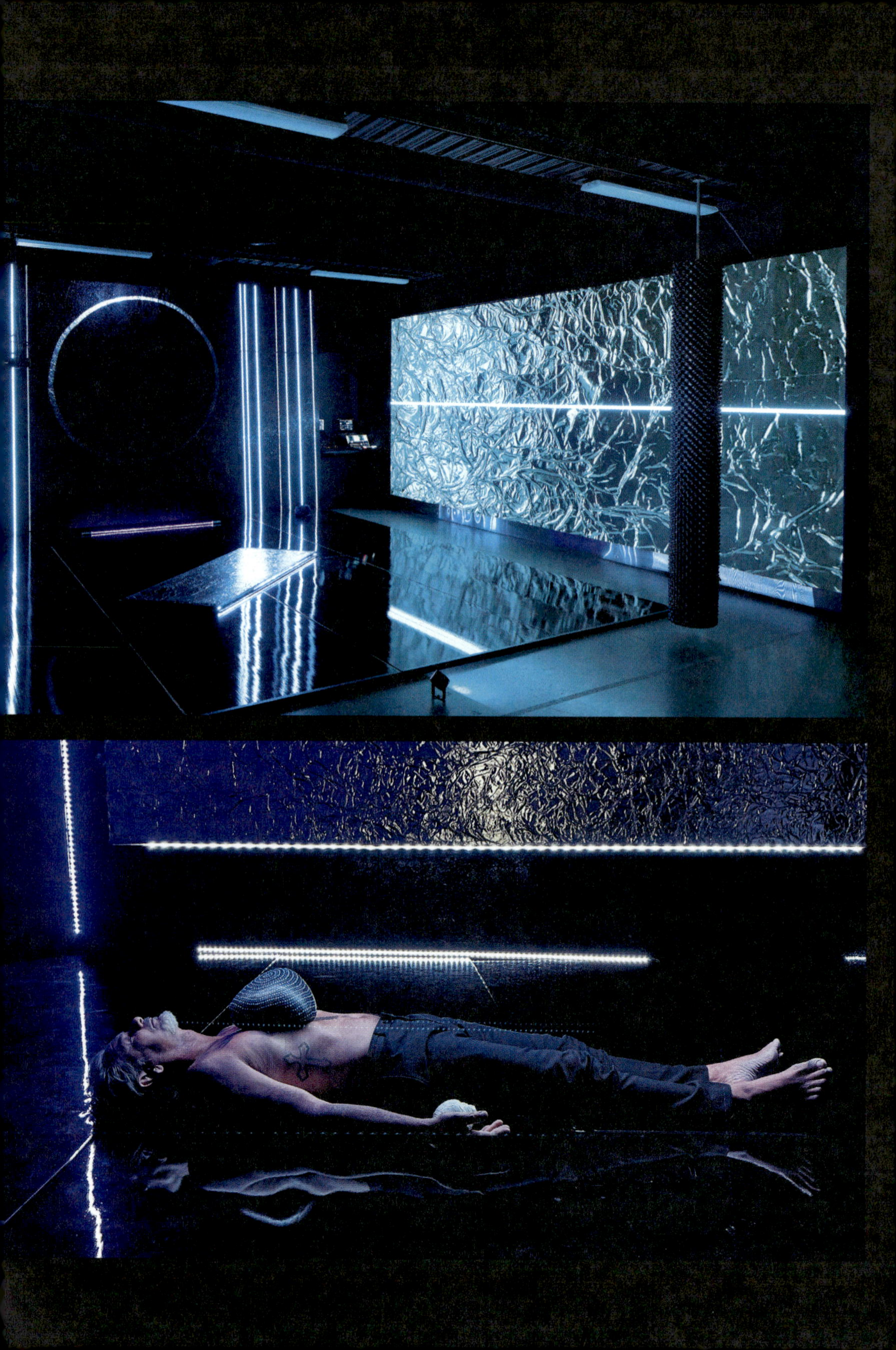

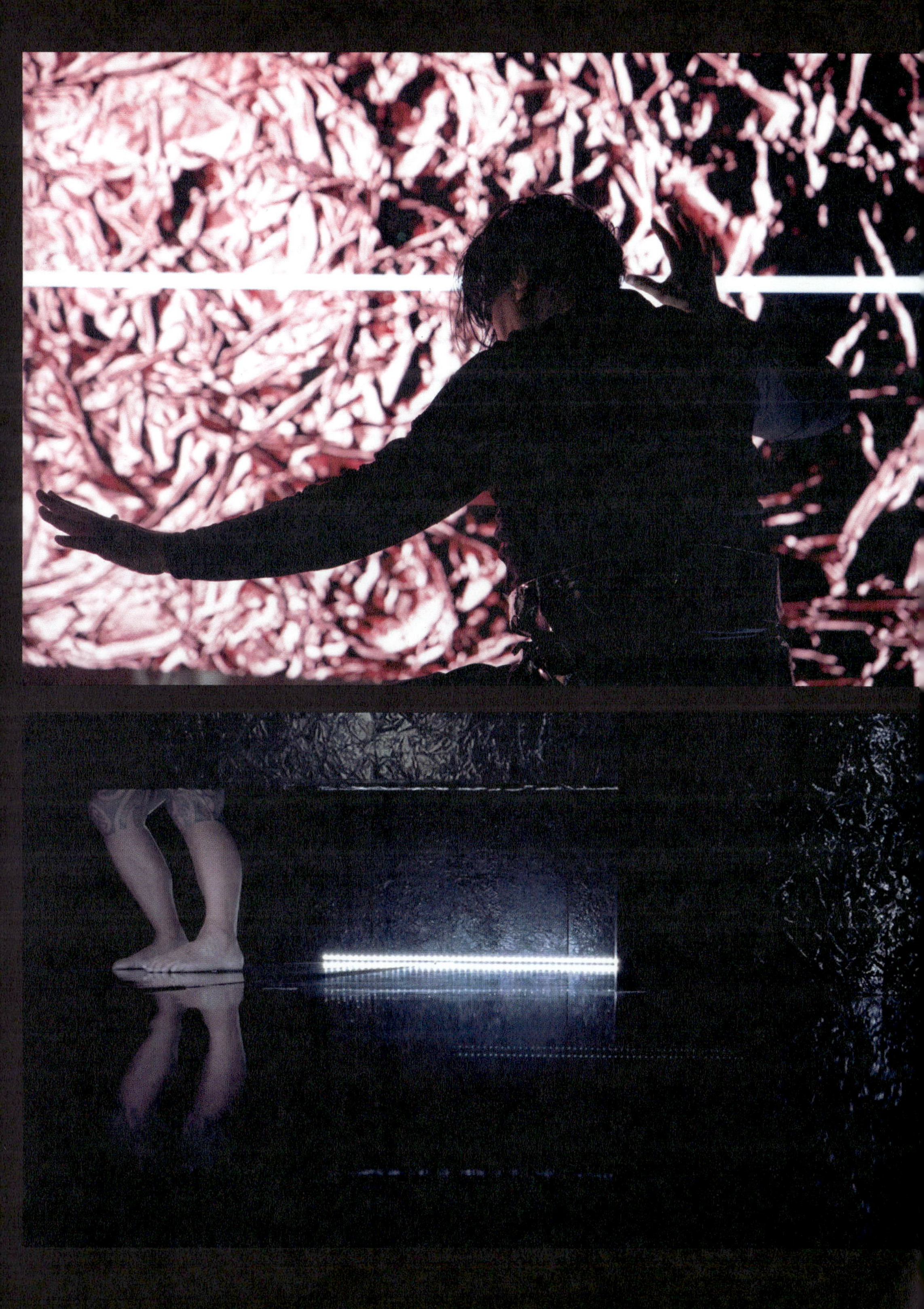

SUPER MASSIVE THUNDER BOOM ULTIMATE COLLECTION

pp. 141–45
Super Massive Thunder Boom Ultimate Collection, presented by Maria Hupfield and the Vera List Center for Art and Politics at Abrons Arts Center, New York, in partnership with Abrons Arts Center and the Center for Imagination in the Borderlands, May 6, 2022. Photos by Argenis Apolinario, courtesy of the Vera List Center for Art and Politics.

MARIA HUPFIELD

ARTIST STATEMENT

At the conclusion of my 2020–2022 Borderlands Fellowship, I presented *Super Massive Thunder Boom Ultimate Collection*, a multiformat performance art event showcasing Indigenous art, design, and song. Bringing together artists and makers in a demonstration of sovereignty and cultural strength, the event was hosted the day after the National Day of Awareness and Action for Missing and Murdered Indigenous Women, Girls, and Gender Diverse people, with performances by: Ange Loft as Master of Ceremonies, the Dime Collective, Dennis RedMoon Darkheem, and Jane Schoolcraft, with a guest appearance by Nicole Wallace. Held at Abrons Arts Center in New York this event was supported by the David Randolph Distinguished Artist-in-Residence Program and the Vera List Center for Art and Politics at The New School, in partnership with Abrons Arts Center and the Center for Imagination in the Borderlands at Arizona State University, on May 6, 2022.

To document this event I invited Akiko Ichikawa, Christen Clifford, and Katherine Carl, three audience members familiar with performance and my art practice in New York, to write about that evening.

Logo designed by Jared Yazzie, OXDX Clothing.

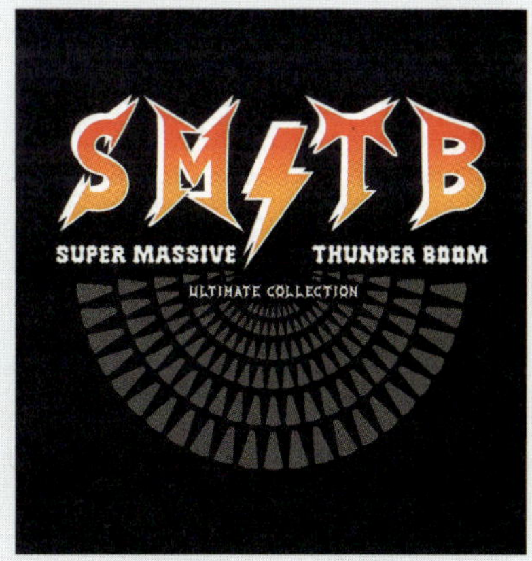

AKIKO ICHIKAWA

THE DIME COLLECTIVE: THE SYMBOLOGY AND GENESIS OF A NAME

On May 6, 2022, First Nations friends Nahka Bertrand, Eruoma Awashish, Sarah Cleary, and artist and translator Sarah Zakaib performed together as the Dime Collective at Abrons Arts Center's Underground Theater. The event was part of an evening entitled *Super Massive Thunder Boom Ultimate Collection*, organized by the Vera List Center and Maria Hupfield, who also mentored the group. I was curious about the symbolism the four employed, emailing them a month after the sold-out night with questions. I heard back from Bertrand, Zakaib, and Cleary, the latter facilitated by Bertrand who brought them all together in Montreal from disparate parts of the Western world. I also conducted additional research online, and this is what I found.

Bertrand and Awashish entered the sold-out affair in regalia they made themselves: Bertrand, who is Dene and French-Canadian, wore a sparkling long coat with fur trim and a ribbon skirt, beating a sacred hand drum made of deerskin. Its sound is believed to resonate between the physical and the invisible worlds; the drum in Anishinaabemowin is called the *taywaygan (tay-way-gan)* meaning the "instrument of the heart." Its reverberation was a call to the human spirit, reproducing a heartbeat. Awashish was in a black-tan skirt, wide regalia belt, and moccasins, her black tank top showing off her arm tattoos, which included a bear claw emblem she often uses in her paintings. Cleary, who is Ilnu from the Mashteuiatsh First Nations reserve of Quebec province, next appeared in a long, dark, flower-print dress (also regalia), holding a fan of eagle feathers, with a white kerchief around her mouth. Zakaib appeared last in a chain-mail mask with feathers around the eye holes, intending to depict a barn owl's eyes. In North American and South African cultures, the bird, with its talent for silence when hunting and flying, is a personification of death and bad luck, but owls in Greek mythology represent Athena, the goddess of handicraft, wisdom, and warfare. Zakaib, who is of Italian-Lebanese descent and based mainly in Rome, intended to convey the more hopeful meaning.

Awashish laid out a floral-patterned kerchief, placing a wrapped object atop it; Cleary sat on an adjacent side, removed her moccasins, and placed the fan on the kerchief. The others looked on, each from the remaining sides: Zakaib with a metal teapot, Bertrand with her back to the audience. After setting the teapot down, Zakaib went to the microphone at stage left and read from the official Italian application form to unbaptize oneself from the Catholic Church, moving to a second microphone stage right and continuing to read. To Bertrand's beating of the taiwaikan, Awashish freed Cleary of her white kerchief.

Awashish then picked up the fan. Eagle feathers are also considered sacred and are used in Indigenous healing ceremonies; they are worn by dancers and are part of their clothing. In First Nations cultures, the eagle is the creature that flies highest in the sky, carrying prayers to the Creator. With the fan, Awashish welcomed the audience and healed the wounds left by residential school.[1] Cleary, whose father is a survivor, told me in French and English, "Dans la performance, nous avons utilisé nos objets de cérémonie pour symboliser la guérison qui doit passer par la réappropriation de nos cultures, de nos valeurs, de notre savoir-faire./We used our ceremonial objects to symbolize the healing that must happen if we want to save our cultures, our values, our know-how." Cleary's

1 The government-sanctioned residential schools in Canada systematically and severally indoctrinated Indigenous children into Euro-Canadian and Christian society, operating from the 1880s into the late twentieth century. The system forcibly separated the children from their families and forbade them from acknowledging or practicing their heritage, culture, and languages.

father tried to take his own life on multiple occasions and, in 1985, went so far as to burn down a church. His daughter shared that she is healing through ceremonies, praying, sobriety, dance, activism, decolonization, reappropriation, and art, as ways to grapple with intergenerational trauma. At Abrons Arts Center, Cleary danced with a small bouquet of irises in hand, dimes embroidered at the ankles of her pants clinking and shimmering.

The performance ended with the four women seated on the flower kerchief serving themselves from the teapot with water, chosen for its convenience, but also its sacredness in Indigenous cultures. By incorporating the daily gesture or action of having tea into the work, Awashish, Cleary, Bertrand, and Zakaib query how to locate the colonial in their daily lives, how it manifests itself, and what it signifies.

The genesis of the Dime Collective's name lies in a conversation Nahka Bertrand had with an Indigenous elder she met at a conference in Vancouver. Both were sitting apart from the conference activities and had been talking at length when they came upon the subject of dimes. "I explained to her that I find a lot of them, and I wanted to ask her if she knew why," Betrand said to me in an email. The elder explained that it meant someone who had passed was thinking about you, adding that she found many as well, especially after the loss of her young grandson, found frozen on a Saskatchewan backroad on New Year's Day. The story of his having seemingly been picked up after a party, driven out a great distance, and left to freeze to death outside, moved the younger conference attendee, a member of the Dene Nation of Denendeh, in the Mackenzie Valley region of Canada's Northwest Territories. "Every time I found a dime, I kept thinking about all our people and how many have been lost and violated, including the thousands of missing and murdered Indigenous women and girls."

Bertrand continued to come upon the coins and collected them. She talked about her new practice with her friend Sarah Zakaib, who is versed in crochet, knitting, hand sewing, and lacemaking. Zakaib suggested they create art with the change; Bertrand, having studied Indigenous theater and performance art, suggested they do so through performance, and Zakaib, too, started to gather dimes. When the Missing and Murdered Indigenous Women (MMIW) phenomenon came to light, the two decided they wanted to make wearable art pieces to give to members of the Indigenous community: the image and symbol of the dime representing not only money, value, and those who have passed, but also colonialism—its face bears the image of Queen Elizabeth II. (Awashish's regalia belt in the Abrons performance included a depiction of the queen's head upside down to indicate Awashish's rejection of her as a figurehead.) In French, *dîmes* also designates the indulgences of the Catholic Church.

The duo tried several times to start their project over the years; after a while, having accumulated stacks of dimes, Bertrand and Zakaib reached out to artist Eruoma Awashish, Bertrand's friend. Awashish, who is Atikamekw and French Canadian, was drawn to the project; she was commissioned in 2021 to paint a mural at the Musée d'art de Joliette in Quebec province in collaboration with the Centre d'amitié autochtone de Lanaudière (Native Friendship Center), in memory of Joyce Echaquan, a thirty-seven-year-old Atikamekw woman who was abused by staff on the floor of a hospital dedicated to her ethnic group in the city of Saint-Charles-Borromée, and died on September 28, 2020, shortly thereafter. Even Prime Minister Justin Trudeau called the incident "another example of systemic racism."

After being contacted by Bertrand and Zakaib about collaborating, Awashish in turn reached out to Sarah Cleary, with whom she had performed in another collective, Trickster Sisters. Cleary joined enthusiastically. The visual artist, pow-wow dancer, and performer had sold reproductions of Awashish's Joliette mural online with her to raise funds to buy art and crafts supplies for Joyce Echaquan's children. Hupfield mentored the four over Zoom on the choice and fabrication of their wearables for the May 2022 performance in New York City.

Undergirding the Dime Collective's ethos is the generative belief in the healing power of art. The group's use of cultural symbols (hand drum, eagle feathers, regalia belts, ribbon skirts, government-issued coinage) are also deliberate acts of deconstruction and reappropriation. As Cleary indicated to me, "We are aware that performance art is a vector of social change; it allows for reflection on society. We take advantage of this medium to disturb (déranger), to heal (guérir), to decolonize (décoloniser), and to reaffirm our vision of the world and our presence on the territory."

CHRISTEN CLIFFORD

BEAUTY AND LOUDNESS

I arrived late to *Super Massive Thunder Boom Ultimate Collection: The Day After Awareness.* I had been at Abortion Stories 2022, an event in Tompkins Square Park. It was May 6, the day after the state legislature of Louisiana approved a bill that states that life begins at the moment of fertilization and declares abortion as homicide. I arrived at Abrons Arts Center angry, wet, cold, and wanting.

"The room is at capacity," the man at the desk told me.

"But I have a ticket reserved."

"Sorry!"

"OK! Can you please tell me, is there a lavatory?" I knew very well where it was, but I wanted to distract him. After I exited the bathroom I walked briskly to the downstairs theater, that wonderful cement half circle, and the usher at the door let me in! Woo hoo!

My mood moved when I walked in and a man was lamenting missing and murdered Indigenous women. A real lament, a passionate expression of sorrow. This event was a "demonstration of sovereignty and cultural strength the day after the National Day of Awareness and Action for Missing and Murdered Indigenous Women, Girls, and Gender Diverse people," the day after the wear-red #mmiwg2s. The man was Dennis RedMoon Darkeem, a Bronx-based artist and educator, Yamassee Creek-Seminole Native American, who danced alone on the stage, a projection of a purpl-blue sky with stars behind him. He was wearing a white headband, the front of his shirt was white with strips of black ribbon running horizontally across his chest and hanging vertically down his torso; the back of his shirt was the inverse, with white ribbon stitched against a black background. The ribbons flowed behind him as he spun around and stretched one hand upward, then the other. His right hand was red, the left hand white. There were red and yellow braids on the stage, an oar, musical instruments. He handed red ribbons to the front row. He lamented as projections of missing and murdered women, girls, and gender diverse people hit the back wall. The last projection read, "THIS IS DEDICATED TO MY STUDENT WHO NEVER MADE IT HOME FROM SCHOOL AND ALL OF THE MISSING INDIGENOUS WOMEN."

Then, Ange Loft, who acted as MC for the evening, read a poem by Jane Schoolcraft—I heard "it all rumbled" and felt it in my bones.

Next, a black banner with white lettering appeared along the back wall: "Jane Schoolcraft,"[1] and Maria Hupfield, dressed in her signature jingle pants made from gray industrial felt and bells, tells the audience about a woman, Jane Schoolcraft, who was a teacher and poet. And then there are four women, three with drums, one with a red electric guitar, who launched into Bikini Kill's 1993 "Rebel Girl"—I was in the back, standing, dancing, and shouting "YES! YES! Aaaaaawwwwwwwoooooo!" and the people in the last row, just in front of me, weren't expecting the yelling in their ears, and I moved back and sung along "Rebel Girl! Rebel Girl! Rebel Girl you are the queen of my world!" Sometimes they are off key, but they are punk, and they get back on and it doesn't matter. They are Clamor. They are Volume. They are Intensity. They are Super. They are Massive. They are Thundering. They Boom.

1 Schoolcraft was the "first [Native American] literary writer, the first known Indian woman writer, the first known Indian poet, the first known poet to write poems in a Native American language, and the first known American Indian to write out traditional Indian stories." Robert Dale Parker, *The Sound the Stars Make Rushing Through the Sky: The Writings of Jane Johnston Schoolcraft* (Philadelphia: University of Pennsylvania Press, 2008), 2.

I feel the revolution in their yelps and beats. I'm dancing and spinning alone in the back—fucking COVID, I haven't seen live music in forever, and here are these Indigenous women inviting us all to join them in their joy and rage. Maria, she's the center, her hair is flying. Now the audience in front is loosening up, we are all singing along, we are together, and here we have the Indigenous Riot grrrl band we didn't know we needed. When they play 1989's "Gouge Away" by The Pixies, I'm grinding to the grunge, "Gouge away, you can gouge away. Stay all day, if you want to." I'm thinking of Samson and Delilah, of heroin, of the destructive force of alcohol in my life.

As Jane Schoolcraft plays, I'm free, fluid, fired up. They are unrestrained, full of anticipation and tension like all great rock bands, and suddenly I think of Martha Wilson's conceptual art band, DISBAND (whose members included, at different times, Ilona Granet, Donna Henes, Ingrid Sischy, Diane Torr, Barbara Ess, and Barbara Kruger). I think of artist Alice Bag's band The Bags, and I think about Ann Magnuson's art bands Vulcan Death Grip and Bongwater, and I think of my own short-lived feminist-performance-art-punk band, Society of the Speculum.[2] Is Jane Schoolcraft a real band or an art band? Is there a difference? Does it matter?

2 Members included Carolina Franco, Cassandra Neyenesch, Dana May Schwister, and myself.

All I know is the feeling, the loudness, the absence of silence. Rebecca Solnit calls silence "the universal condition of oppression."[3] When I hear Jane Schoolcraft's Lisa Myers's crunchy guitar, I think of the Indigenous singer Arigon Starr and "The Salmon Song," a punk anthem from twenty years ago, with its catchy refrain "I! Will! Come! Back!"

3 Rebecca Solnit, "A Short History of Silence," *The Mother of All Questions* (Chicago: Haymarket Books, 2017), 24.

When they play AC/DC's 1990 "Thunderstruck," I hear women singing and hitting those metal strings and skin drums to “Sound of the drums, Beating in my he-ar-art” and “We’re doing fine fine fine Thunderstruck.” I think of Walter De Maria’s 1977 *Lightning Field* in New Mexico. I think of being shocked. I notice they are all wearing black T-shirts with a fiery logo “SM/TB” as a play on AC/DC’s logo (a lightning bolt in place of a slash). Hupfield yelps and howls to the guitar riffs and hyper drumming that ends the show. The crowd yelps and howls and claps.

Later, I learned from the program that “Jane Schoolcraft is a three-member performance art band based in Toronto, members include artists, curators, and Indigenous academics, Lisa Myers on guitar, Mikinaak Migwans and Maria Hupfield on vocals and hand drums.”

Lisa Myers (guitar), Mikinaak Migwans (drum and vocals), Nicole Wallace (guest drummer on “Rebel Girl”) and Maria Hupfield (drum and vocals) are volcanoes; they are feminist solidarity combining Native and non-Native feminisms with traditionally masculine rock.

Jane Schoolcraft is a respite and a provocation, a balm and an invocation; a kick-ass reminder that we can’t do anything alone.

As I walk back into the rain, I’m stronger, full of the power of this evening. My blood sings, like a heart towards the river, a comfort shining and raging.

KATHERINE CARL

DOCUMENTATION OF PERFORMANCE

Gathering is one of many ways to be physically present for this performance—a beautiful hinge experience.

The invitation to write and reflect, which came later, is a collaboration in contributing to the legacy of the work.

(This performance, with integrity, forges social creation and cultural sustenance.)

***

The gathering thunder
The hinge that invites

Many genres

Bullhorn

Specific objects

Wrapped mouth
Friend, woman unwraps, is she an ancestor is she a missing woman
Intense movement and singing
Dimes
Tea
Circling in the dimes performance
The rhythm of comfort and fortitude. The visceral memory

The feathers, the smudge, the ornate over the top costumes
Being wrapped like a mummy coming back to life the

words, the guts of forceful bodily language to dance it out, stomp it out, anger, eyes flashing, smudge it out, renew the air, renew the bodily movements, renew the voice. Tough, firm. Veil, balaclava, ancestor, glittering. Alluring, movie-star feathers, and sequins.

The clink clink clink of dimes, dropping, meditatively, dropping, clinking, then pouring flowing like water like oil scattering, glittering, exude, get out. Discarded dimes. Just ornament, empty, just glitz.

The tender calming tea, connecting, resting, sitting, lounging, feeling the cloth underneath the legs, feeling the warm tea moving into the stomach, feeling the warm looks and soft smiles one to each other. No words needed, for now. Serene. Rest, for now.

Gathering, reciprocal. Among the women together around the cloth and objects. That serenity wafts through the theater and envelops all of us with comfort.

The hinge experience, the relay, our distinct backgrounds connect at a particular moment, and then disperse again but carry this memory of this gathering on our journey.

Oar, bells, shakers, move, angular
black and white stripes.
Ribbons on shirt, ribbons on bullhorn
Ceremony
Projections

Return to safety integrity land.
Get rid of the oil boom that has ravaged women
Industry and destruction driven by money.

The Thunder Boom gathers the power the might the loudness and fury and celebration of life and bonds that protect one another. The massive loud booms drive away—and for a time can replace—the sorrow with this fierce force that rises from deep within and spreads out.

The ultimate collection—gathering together as a force for protection and stamina.

Lots of rock-and-roll glitz, bling for fun. Maria's jingly pants recall bullets—cones of thinly rolled metal reused as a fun object that individually seems silly and innocuous and decorative but in formation, in multitude, and in movement become raucous and loud. The drums make a lot of noise, but it is not chaotic; they have a determined rhythm. The beat is a grounding heartbeat, a walking pace for a footpath. No false moves, but not rigid.
Jovial, fierce, and lightening with levity and leavening.
Informal but thoughtful with seriousness and meaning.
There are heavy reasons for being here, but we leave with a feeling of lightness and power.

The day after the mourning, grief, horror, sickening
Then comes the roar, the stamina, the propulsion to overcome this violence and terror.
Energy is not expended but compounded.

What *is* the material of the jingles?

The Thunder BOOM of women's presence of firmness
Instead of the oil boom, the oil money that is fueling so much of the violence against women. Instead, is the thunder boom of strength, power, protection, presence, and firmness, standing for selves, for safety, for life.

Exuberance of learning.
Reworking something you thought you knew. Layering together elements that were previously disjointed in a new way. Areas that somehow always left me with questions, things that didn't make sense.
Showing, gathering, up, attending to, legacies,

feelings, pride, power, shifts.
Shift of perspective-sharing this rebelling in this—
this is decolonization in practice
Pocket relay

Accumulation of memory placed in a powerful well-
spring for each woman one dream dime at a time.

Deliberate actions
Specific objects

Settings
Expectations
Tools
Conditions

Land and people

Firmness
Power
Boom

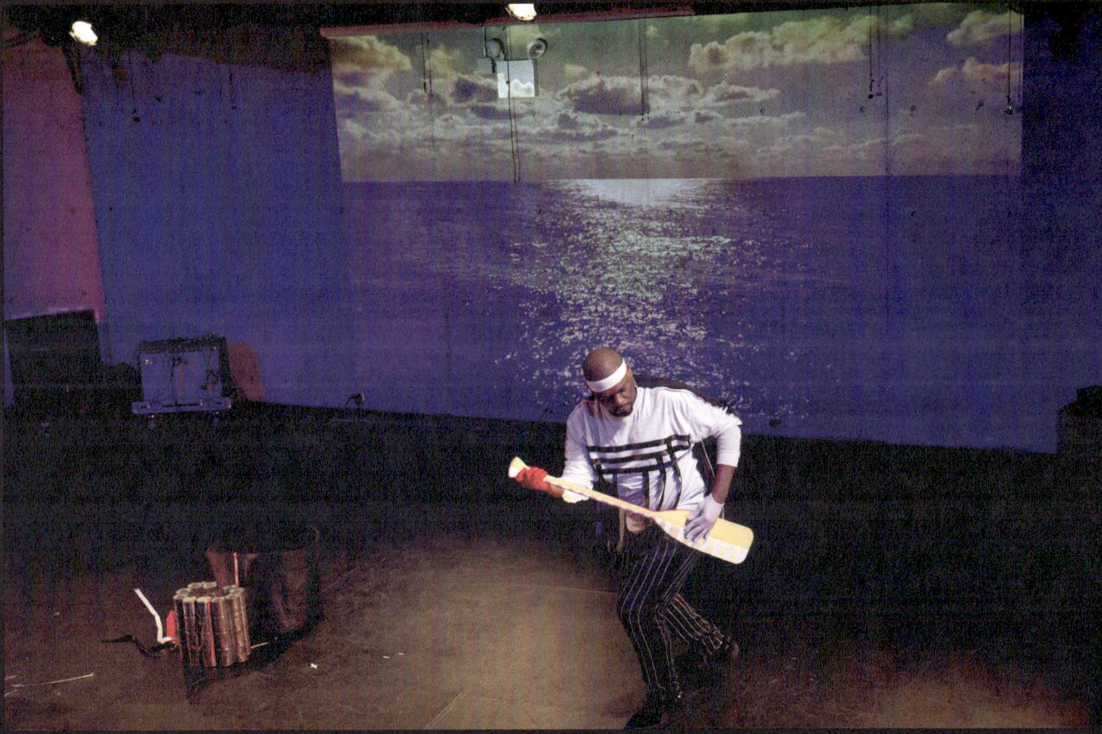

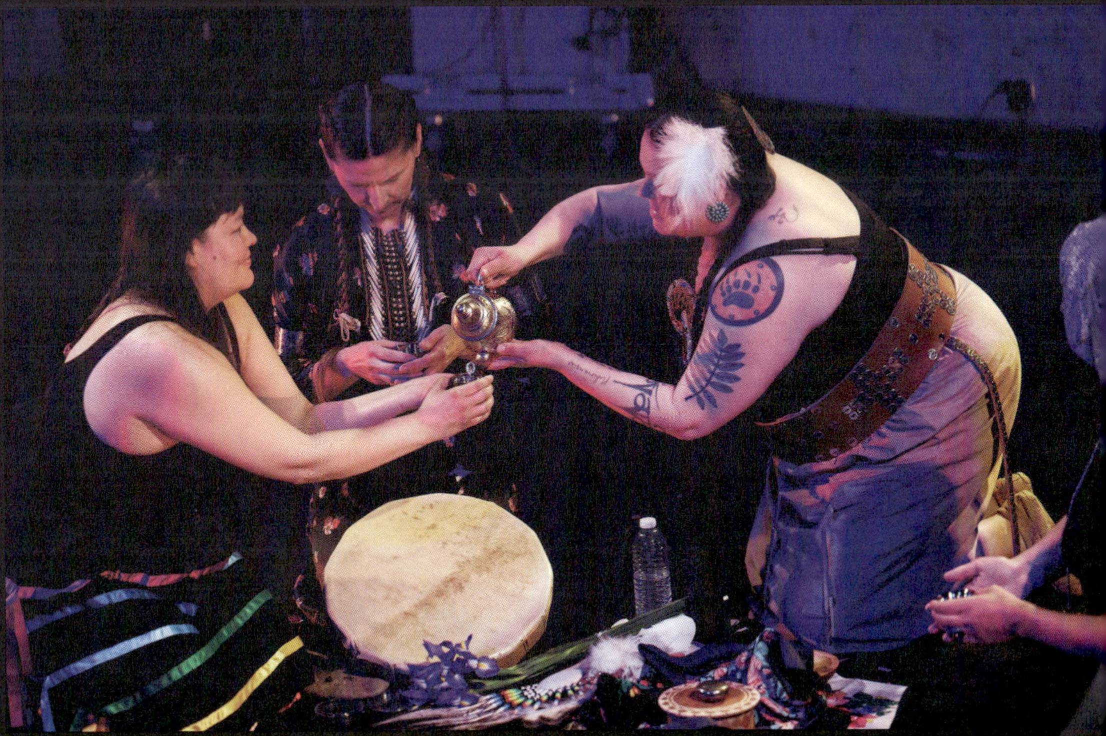

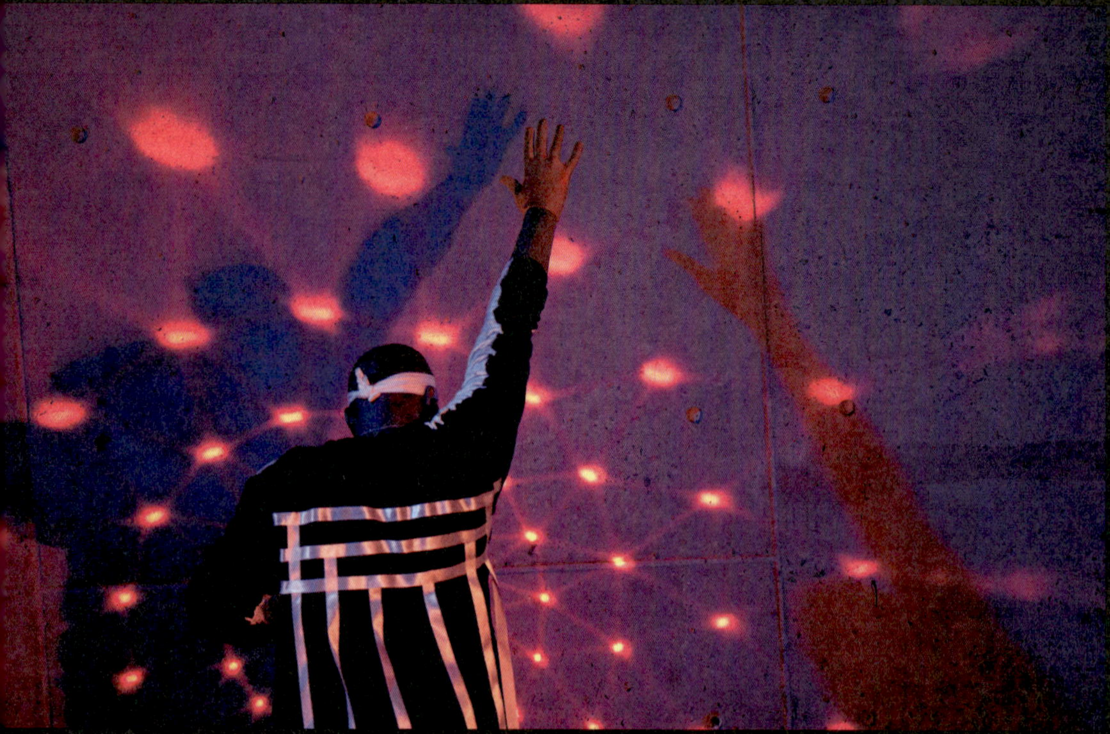

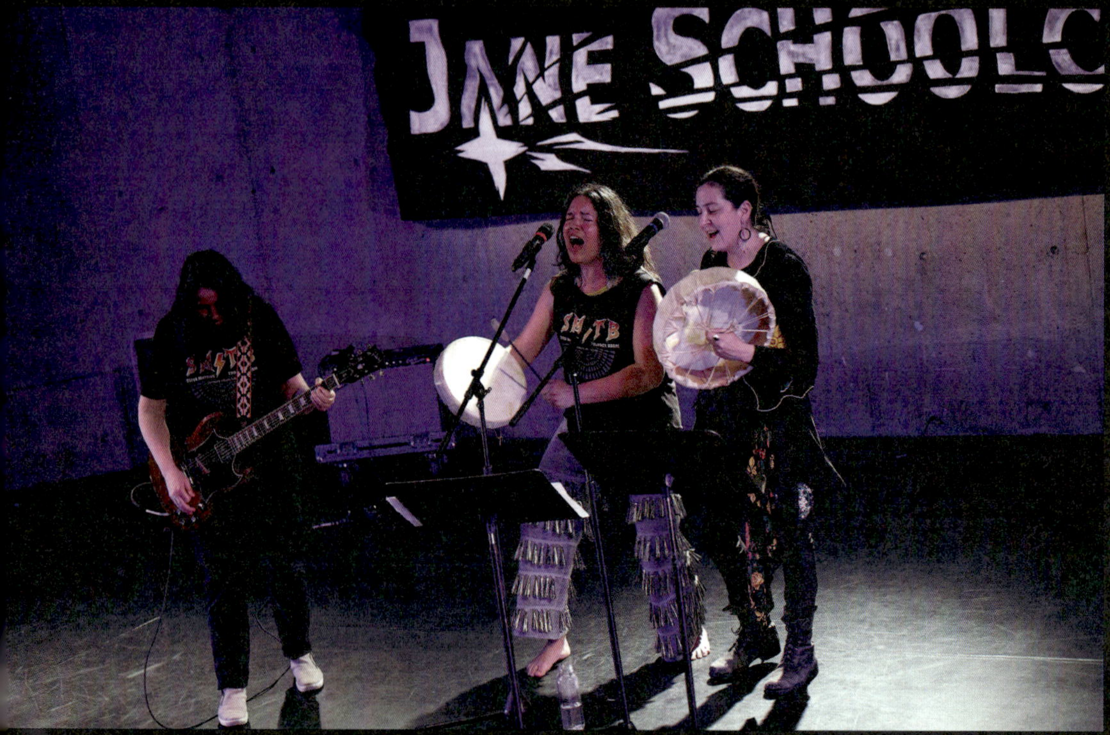

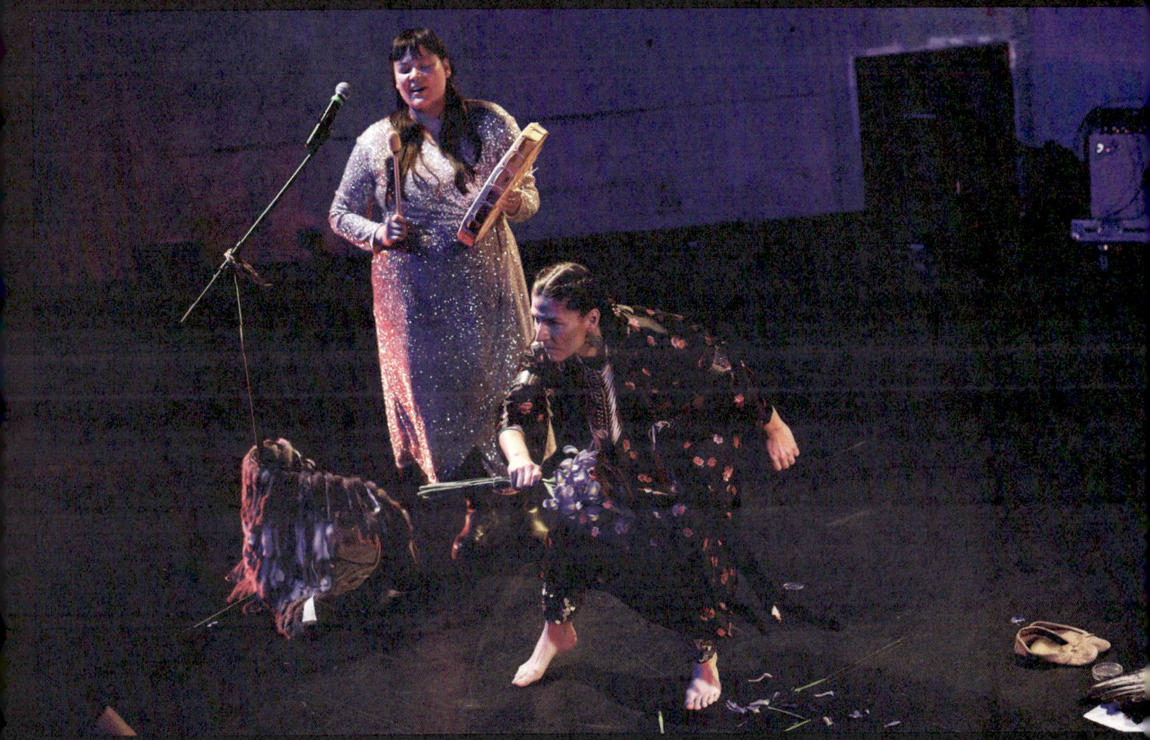

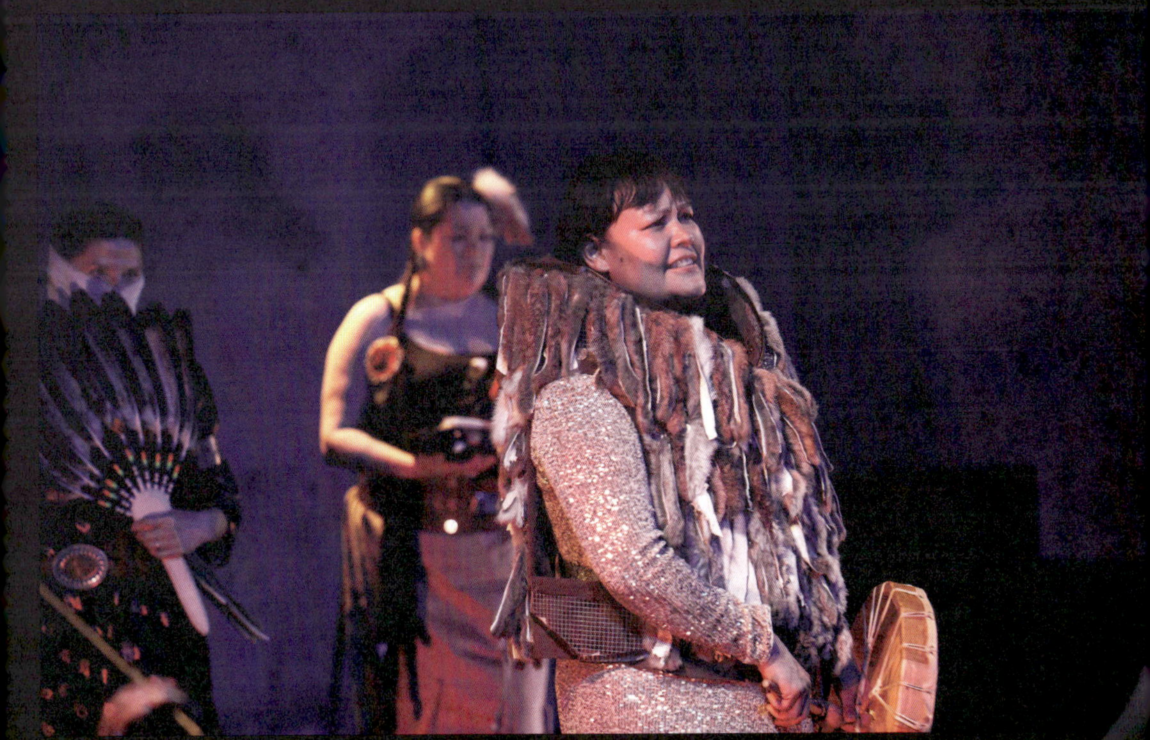

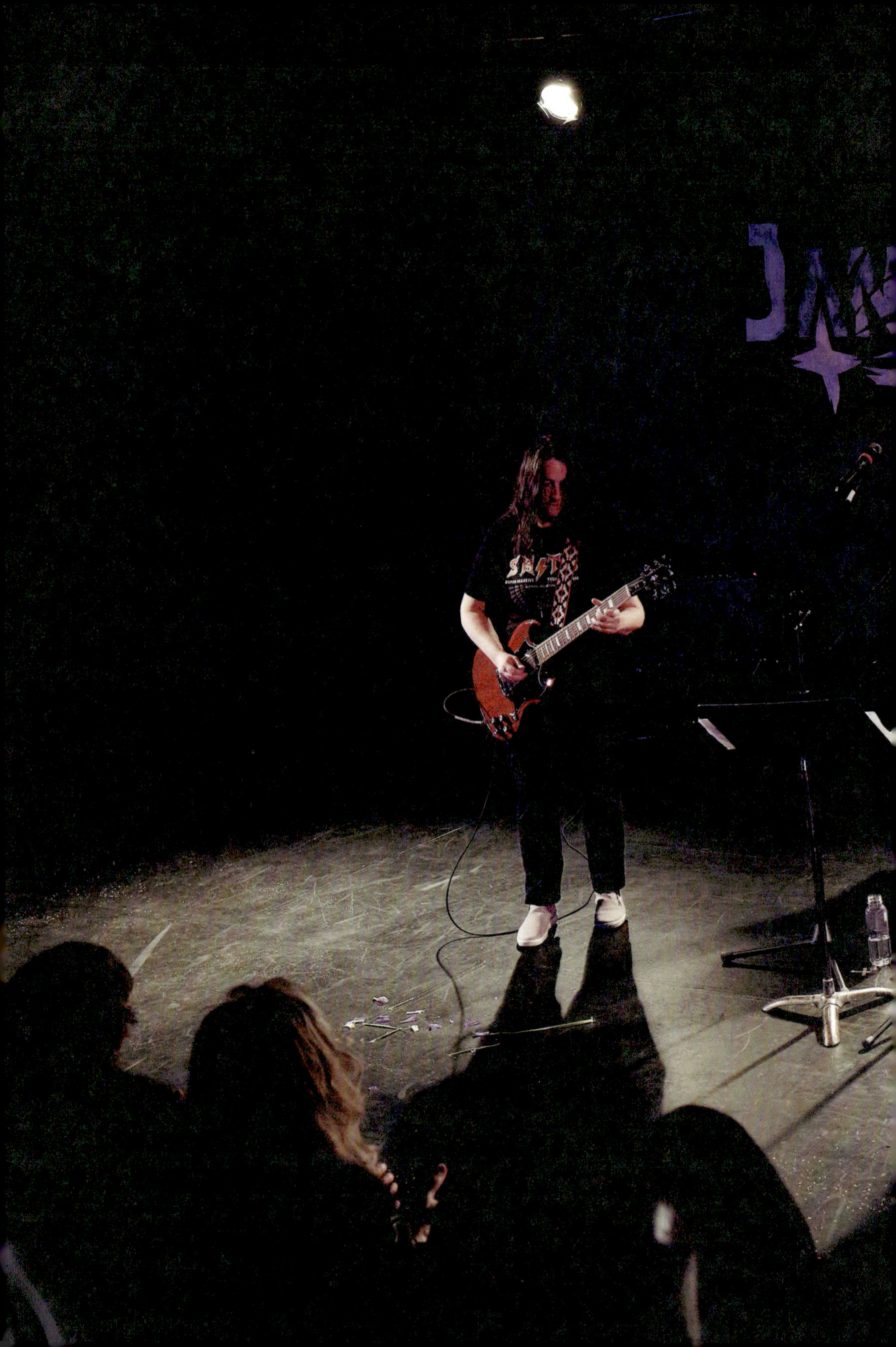

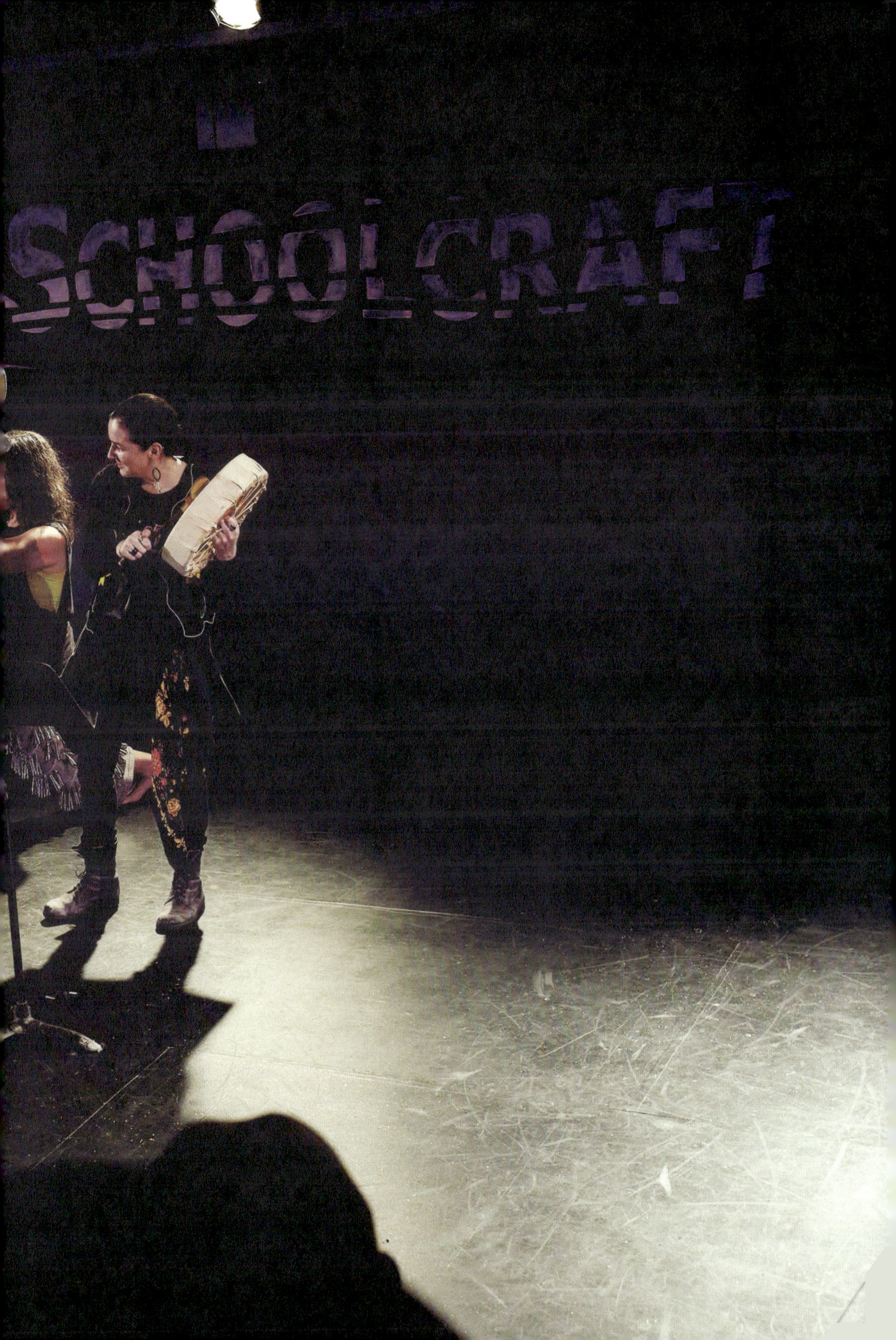
SCHOOLCRAFT

RE’AL CHRISTIAN

ALL VISIBLE DIRECTIONS: MARIA HUPFIELD AND NATALIE DIAZ

Weaving through movement, sound, text, and touch, *All Visible Directions Between Sky and Water* mediates a gap between the body and the land. In an experimental dialogue-as-performance, Maria Hupfield and Natalie Diaz consider the liminal space of the horizon, which Diaz defines as "a place of perceptual exchange … a width of a line … a wilderness.… Its immeasurability, the largeness of its perspective and sensuality have been things non-Indigenous people have felt the need and fear to try and contain with a boundary, a line marking up and down, light and day, eventually all meaning good or bad."[1] Together, Hupfield and Diaz expand their thinking on this non-dualistic space, a site of coexistence between endings and beginnings, sky and land, land and body.

1 Vera List Center for Art and Politics, "All Visible Directions Between Sky and Water with Natalie Diaz and Maria Hupfield," December 12, 2022. https://www.veralistcenter.org/events/all-visible-directions-between-sky-and-water-with-natalie-diaz-and-maria-hupfield.

The performance took place in The New School's historic Orozco Room, the home of Mexican artist José Clemente Orozco's five-part fresco murals, including *Table of Universal Brotherhood*. Commissioned in 1931, the murals touch on themes of labor, enslavement, immigration, family, community, political action, and progress, a fitting backdrop for the performance. Diaz and Hupfield begin with a simple call and response:

"What's this?" "Is this sky? I am sky." "I am sky." "I am water." "I am water." "I am water." "I am water." "I am sky." "I am sky." "I am sky." "I am sky." "I am water." "I am sky." "I am water." "I am sky … I am water." "I am sky." "I am sky." "I am water." "You are water." "Am I water?" "You are water." "You are sky." "I am sky." "If we are touching, what am I? … Are we still touching?"

Their speech is punctuated by rhythmic pauses; each interval is accompanied by a physical gesture—with each movement, their arms and hands periodically touch as they echo one another's gestures, creating a chorus of verbal and nonverbal exchanges. Their string of questions and assertions slowly forge an abstract dialogue into being. "If sky touches water, what is it?" "What's between?" "Is what's between also what's outside?" "Yes." "Are we both inside?" "Yes." "Am I also inside?" "Yes." "Is there a middle?" "Yes." Here, the horizon emerges as the answer to a riddle, one that underscores the inseparability of the space where land and sky meet. Intertwining language and limbs, their individual bodies, like the horizon itself, become entangled and fluid.

They then shift their attention to the audience, opening their call and response to those in attendance, beginning with several people they know. Hupfield weaves around the room, asking individuals if they have stories about the sky. One such exchange was with her husband, artist Jason Lujan: "Do you have a story about sky that comes from the desert that you want to share?" "No." "No?" "No." "You don't have a story about the sky that comes from the desert?" "No." "You have a story but you don't want to tell me the story, is this correct?" "Yes." "Who is the story for?" "Us." "Who is *us*?" "*Nde*." "Am I nde?" "No." "If I'm not nde, is your story about sky from the desert for me?" "No." "Thank you."

In the third part of the performance, Hupfield introduces a pair of jingle-covered felt boots. Jingles, as she has pointed out, are distinct from bells as they have no internal mechanism with which they can make a sound—they are silent until struck by other jingles, they can only make sound collectively. As Hupfield moves fluidly with the jingles, striking, shaking, waving them with varying degrees of strength and rigidity, Diaz speaks to their shared thinking on the notion of the horizon, place, space, language, and image.

> How do we think of space and place in the context of a body? The horizon has been a question for us, the idea that the earth meets the sky—naturally,

> you think of a meeting as two separate things coming together. What if those things have never been separate? What if instead, we are thinking about a singular energy, or an entanglement, or a single body? How do you create space with the body if you take away the idea of place? Not place itself, but all the things place has been. And how does language work in that new place of body. How does touch work. How do we think about a word like "horizon," like "meeting," like "border." The idea of a border only exists because there are bodies that can cross it. There is touch that makes that border possible. Therefore, a border is impossible.[2]

2 Partially paraphrased by author.

The horizon, or rather the impossibility of it, becomes a metaphor for a body that exists beyond the limits or context of space. As Diaz notes, the horizon exemplifies the myriad ways in which the Indigenous body has had to become place in and of itself because of the colonization and continued occupation of native land. Through their performance, Hupfield and Diaz form an alliance through mutual recognition of one another as Indigenous women from across cultures, geographies, and language to share the same space. Their encounter with one another and with the audience signals the ability of the Indigenous body to see from more than one point of view, a version of what W. E. B. Du Bois called a "double consciousness,"[3] or the multiplicity of understanding oneself from the perspective of another. As Hupfield and Diaz embody the horizon, it manifests not as a border, but a borderland. In the words of Chicana scholar Gloria Alzaldúa, "A border is a dividing line, a narrow strip along a steep edge. A borderland is a vague and undetermined place created by the emotional residue of an unnatural boundary. It is in a constant state of transition."[4] Thinking through borderlands in this context, we

3 W. E. B. Du Bois, The Souls of Black Folk (Chicago: A. C. McClurg & Co., 1903).

4 Gloria Anzaldúa, *Borderlands/ La Frontera: The New Mestiza* (San Francisco: Aunt Lute Books, 1999), 3.

must ask: What happens when you take away place as a symbol of Indigeneity and erasure? What happens when an Indigenous body has to become place when the land is occupied and compromised?

Writing about a performance five years after it took place puts many things into context. First, the conversation between Maria Hupfield and Natalie Diaz at the Vera List Center—with one another and with those in attendance—was one of the seeds that generated the Borderlands Fellowship, which launched two years later. Secondly, in extending this conversation to the audience, Hupfield and Diaz open new possibilities of mishearing and misrecognition, and thus opportunities for learning from one another. Their performance might be seen as a rehearsal for a different mode of addressing a familiar topic, and in navigating difference, one can uncover the intricacies, subtleties, mishearings, and misunderstandings inherent in language as a singular form of communication.

Lastly, the performance embodies the ways in which Indigenous protocols of close listening, of sharing and holding space, of respecting one’s separation from an “us,” and of recognizing the other can allow us to better understand our own relation to the world. Thinking alongside these protocols, we can consider the body in the context of land, connected through a shared energy. With this, we return to the horizon, where earth meets sky as a singular entity, unbordered, like two hands gesturing toward one another in space.

CARIN KUONI

BREAKING PROTOCOL. AFTERWORD

The book you are holding is printed on 100 percent PCW–FSC certified paper produced by Rolland in Saint-Jérôme, in an area commonly known as Québec, using 93 percent biogas delivered via an eight-mile pipeline from a landfill nearby. From the paper mill it was shipped by rail to Winnipeg and from Winnipeg by truck to Friesens, the employee-owned printer in Altona, Manitoba. In Altona, Friesens used 100 percent vegetable based inks—cyan, magenta, yellow, and black—manufactured through the triumph max process by Sun Chemical and delivered to Friesens via truck. Nearly all of Friesens' electricity is purchased through MB Hydro which means renewable hydroelectric power. They do have a couple of backup gas generators that are occasionally used, but their impact is minimal. The total GHG emissions from MB Hydro in 2020 were 0.44 tonnes C02e/GWh (the average of neighboring regions is 750). Friesens used sheetfed offset to print the pages and thread to sew them into books. The covers were attached with glue. From Altona, the books were delivered via LTL carrier to our distributor's warehouse in what is today referred to as Tennessee. From there, the books were sent via the United States Postal Service to bookstores as well as to wholesalers' warehouses such as bookshop.org from which you may have ordered yours. Some copies came directly to the Vera List Center office at The New School in Lenapehoking in order to be redistributed: we've sent them out via USPS in envelopes padded with 100 percent post-consumer recycled content.

Breaking Protocol, in other words, is assembled of parts that have traversed vast distances, guided and nurtured by many people. Now that it's constructed, like a vessel in high waters, the book also holds and protects within its pages words, images, documents, and thoughts by twenty-eight extraordinary people, most of them Indigenous performance artists and all of them invited by artist Maria Hupfield. Hupfield is building within the physical confines of the book a space of kinship and sharing, at a moment of pandemic loss, grief, and pause, as well as survivance.

At the Vera List Center, we have had the joy of observing and learning from Hupfield, accompanying and supporting her fellowship project

Breaking Protocol, and seeing how she adapted it to a pandemic context. The VLC occupies part of the unceded territory of the Lenape nation. We are not an Indigenous-led organization, but we are continuously trying to understand how the center functions in the world and what it means to nurture communities of politically engaged artists. We keep asking ourselves: What is the political agency of an aesthetic practice? How can we help shape a truly “new” school and offer opportunities for peer learning? How can we support forms of knowledge building that are not meant for us? How can we be allies to Indigenous positions when we come from a compromised institutional presence? How do we prefigure political and social justice in our own daily practice?

Explicitly—or not—protocols determine much of what we do. They are a bit like language, they organize how we relate to each other, to our cultural, social, and political environments, and to the beings and technologies that shape them. In seeking answers to some of the questions above, we dedicated our biennial focus theme to protocols and called it *As for Protocols*. We want to make protocols of engagement more visible, more explicit, more inclusive, and hopefully, more just. Hupfield’s *Breaking Protocol* has been an important guiding post in this collective research.

It helps to acknowledge who you are and who you are not. The quality and precision of the invitation to engage is also decisive. Protocols can help clarify who is invited, who is not, and who is invited to do what. The Coffee Break sessions that originated this book took place in privacy. The VLC team set them up, but that space of encounter was inaccessible to us. Invitations were issued, meetings set, gifts exchanged, no recording and no photograph emerged to meet conventional desires for documentation. The Coffee Breaks, all six of them, came and went.

A year later, *Breaking Protocol* has assembled diverse statements on performance generated in the Coffee Break sessions. And like those conversations, *Breaking Protocol* is an organic exchange guided by Hupfield. There is no sequential order to the contributions—they are not alphabetical, nor sorted by medium, seniority, or region. Echoing the Coffee Break sessions themselves, the book’s organizing principle is kinship. Like the material components that comprise it, its content is an assemblage of voices from different locations, people of a shared place wherever they may be. Many of the artists have worked together before; you've noticed how they reference one another throughout their conversations, creating a kind of map tracing lineages of community, collaboration, and relationality. Little surprise that such kinship is expressed in especially meaningful ways through performance—a medium that centers a precise moment or location of address for both the speaker and the listener to be in the world together. When anthropologist Audra Simpson describes Mohawk kinship, she points to the opening statement (almost a protocol), "This is how I am to you."[1] The explicit naming of a relationship emphasizes its dynamic quality, not its fixed points: This is *how* I am to you, not who I am to you. And, again after Simpson, "kinship is made material through dialogue and discourse."[2] When she speaks of reservations as sites of ongoing permanence as well as mobility, once more a performativity is implied. Could Simpson's "refusal to be enfolded into state logic"[3] find its enactment in Indigenous performance that transcends geographical distance? And if so, what are the protocols that can be shared and learned from Indigenous performance artists?

It is a fitting decree that *Breaking Protocol* developed as part of Hupfield's Borderlands Fellowship. A joint initiative between the VLC and the Center for Imagination in the Borderlands at Arizona State University, the fellowship applies an Indigenous lens to considerations of borders and, foremost, undermines the legitimacy and authority of the nation state and its adjacent borders. This book does the same, but as a vessel it creates a safe space, inviting others in, all while maintaining and celebrating specificities. In her introduction, Hupfield predicts pleasure and joy to the last drop of this book. *Breaking Protocol*, including its binding, cover, and material aspects, are offered here with humility and gratitude.

1 Audra Simpson, *Mohawk Interruptus. Political Life Across the Borders of Settler States* (Durham, North Carolina: Duke University Press, 2014), 15.

2 Ibid, 9.

3 Ibid, 185.

ACKNOWLEDGMENTS

We are grateful to many. Foremost our thanks and admiration go to Maria Hupfield. Maria is one of two inaugural Borderlands Fellows, and over the course of two years, from 2020 to 2022, we have learned with and alongside her, witnessing and supporting performances, conversations, gatherings, and now this artist's book. We thank her for her generosity, kindness, and good spirit in times when the pandemic wreaked havoc with our lives.

The Borderlands Fellowship is a joint initiative between the Center for Imagination in the Borderlands (CIB) at Arizona State University and the Vera List Center for Art and Politics (VLC) at The New School. The fellowships are awarded biennially to two artists or scholars to support research projects that create communities across different geographical, cultural, and political landscapes. Each project focuses on the relevance of place, reflecting on questions of borderlands through an Indigenous lens. Guided by the vision of fellowship co-director Natalie Diaz, the Borderlands initiative provides an arc of joint research, encounters, and experiences set in motion by two related projects reflecting on notions of place. We are indebted to Natalie for her support, encouragement, and friendship, and her gentle touches until the very last moments of the book's development. Her work and the Center for Imagination in the Borderlands are shining lights guiding us. We also thank her team at CIB, especially Program Manager Gionni Ponce.

It is a pleasure to recognize the circle of experts who advised us in developing the Borderlands Fellowship and assisted with nominations and the selection in the inaugural cycle. They are Heather Ahtone, Raven Chacon, Jaskiran Dhillon, Nick Estes, Maritza Estrada, Carolina Fernandez, Elizabeth Grady, Christopher Green, Casandra Hernandez, Richard William Hill, Candice Hopkins, Layli Long Soldier, Cannupa Hanska Luger, Kevin Martinez, Alan Michelson, Julio Morales, Wanda Nanibush, Laura Ortman, Eriola Pira, Jolene Rickard, Paul Chaat

Smith, Mary Stephens, Radhika Subramaniam, Amanda Tachine, Jorge Torres, and Mario Ybara.

Breaking Protocol is witness to exuberant, vital performance practices gathered in challenging times. We are deeply gratful to the contributors who were invited by Maria Hupfield. They are Jackson 2bears, Rebecca Belmore, Lori Blondeau, Pelenakeke Brown, Katherine Carl, Re'al Christian, Christen Clifford, TJ Cuthand, Raven Davis, Vanessa Dion Fletcher, Candice Hopkins, Akiko Ichikawa, Kite, Charles Koroneho, Cheryl L'Hirondelle, Gabrielle L'Hirondelle Hill, Ursula Johnson, Tanya Lukin Linklater, Cathy Mattes, Meagan Musseau, Wanda Nanibush, Peter Morin, Archer Pechawis, Rosanna Raymond, Skeena Reece, Georgiana Uhlyarik, Charlene Vickers, and Laakkuluk Williamson Bathory. Re'al Christian, VLC Assistant Director of Editorial Initiatives, managed the book and edited the contributions masterfully and worked with Amanda Berardi, Research Assistant for the Indigenous Virtual Living Archive, Indigenous Creation Studio, University of Toronto Mississauga, to provide short introductions to the visual essays. The original Coffee Break sessions and the *Super Massive Thunder Boom Ultimate Collection* were organized by VLC Curator and Director of Programs Eriola Pira and expertly facilitated by Director of Operations and Budget Adrienne Umeh. Aryana Ghazi Hessami, PhD candidate in Anthropology at The New School for Social Research, provided additional support during the Coffee Break gatherings. We are grateful to Inventory Press, especially principals Shannon Harvey and Adam Michaels as well as Project Manager Mary Thompson, and their design team at IN-FO.CO, particularly Ella Gold, for a book that captures so well the spirit of collaboration and the energy of performance. It's been an immense pleasure to work with them, and we appreciate their care and sensitivity. And the introduction to the extraordinary printers at Friesens! The Center for Imagination in the Borderlands has supported the production of the book and we're grateful to publish it in association with the CIB. Additional support for the Indigenous-focused programs at the VLC is provided by the Native Arts and Cultures Foundation.

Through initiatives such as the Borderlands Fellowship, the VLC community is continuously growing and our experiences with it. The core team behind the VLC encompasses the VLC staff, board, and The New School. The staff comprises Tabor Banquer, Director of Strategy and Advancement; Re'al Christian, Assistant Director of Editorial Initiatives; Camila Palomino, Curatorial Assistant; Eriola Pira, Curator and Director of Programs; and Adrienne Umeh, Director of Operations and Budget; and myself, Carin Kuoni, Senior Director/Chief Curator.

The VLC board is chaired with a steady, generous hand by James Keith (JK) Brown, assisted by Vice Chair Megan E. Noh and Secretary Norman Kleeblatt. Susan Hapgood was an enthusiastic Board Companion to Maria Hupfield. Before joining the board, Alan Michelson several years ago co-curated *Indigenous New York* with the Vera List Center, a generative program initiative in 2016. He was joined by Jackson Polys, who has since become a Borderlands Advisor. The entire board is our backing and foundation, and we thank everyone: Ujju Aggarwal, Frances Beatty, Linda Earle, Marilyn Greene, Aryana Ghazi Hessami, Pia Infante, Jane Lombard, Susan Meiselas, Naeem Mohaiemen, Mendi + Keith Obadike, Nancy Delman Portnoy, Silvia Rocciolo, and Mary Watson, the Executive Dean of the Schools of Public Engagement at The New School, our academic and intellectual home.

At the VLC, we recognize that our work and assembly spaces occupy the unceded territory of the Lenape Nation. We acknowledge the Lenape as the stewards of this land, recognize their long history of welcoming many nations to Lenapehoking, and pay respect to their ancestors past, present, and future. We are aware of the ongoing oppression of lands, cultures, and the peoples who have inhabited this continental land mass long before European settlers invaded. We turn to the arts and support Indigenous-centered programming such as the Borderlands initiative in the hope that our work contributes to decolonization and anti-racism, to healing, and a more just and equitable future for all.

Gizhemnido
Miigwech gdigo maadiziwin
giimmzhiyaang
Naadamoshinaang wiiwiingewzi-
yaang ensa giizhigak
Miigwech nbaa giizis, osh-
kaabewis giizis, ashiikii-kwe,
gichi-manido.
Miigwech gaamiizhiyaang
maanda Anishinaabemowin
wiignoongoyin

—Maria Hupfield

Breaking Protocol
is co-published by

Inventory Press
2305 Hyperion Ave
Los Angeles, CA 90027
inventorypress.com

Vera List Center for Art and Politics
The New School
66 West 12th Street, Room 604
New York, NY 10011
veralistcenter.org

Editor: Maria Hupfield
Managing editors: Re'al Christian
and Carin Kuoni
Editorial assistant: Amanda Berardi
Copy editor: Re'al Christian
Proofreader: Eugenia Bell
Design: IN-FO.CO
(Adam Michaels, Ella Gold)
Production: Matthew Harvey
Color separations: Thomas Bollier
Printed in Canada by Friesens

ISBN: 9781941753576
LCCN: 2023932300

Cover: Maria Hupfield, *Jingle Spiral*, 2015. Tin jingles on industrial felt, 70 × 70 × 1 inches (178 × 178 × 3 centimeters). Collection Musée des beaux-arts de Montréal, Canada. Image courtesy of the artist.

Distributed by
ARTBOOK | D.A.P.
75 Broad St, Suite 630
New York, NY 10004
artbook.com

Breaking Protocol is published on the occasion of Maria Hupfield's 2020–2022 Borderlands Fellowship, with research, production, editorial, and curatorial support provided by the Vera List Center for Art and Politics at The New School and the Center for Imagination in the Borderlands at Arizona State University. It is published by Inventory Press and the Vera List Center for Art and Politics in association with the Center for Imagination in the Borderlands.

The publication of *Breaking Protocol* has been made possible by the Vera List Center Board and support from the Center for Imagination in the Borderlands. It has also been supported, in part, by The Andy Warhol Foundation for the Visual Arts, the Ford Foundation, the Kettering Fund, and The New School. Additional funding has been provided to the VLC by the Native Arts and Cultures Foundation.